ROOKIE to RETIREMENT

ROOKIE to RETIREMENT

Volume 1

Brian Waugh

Library of Congress Control Number: 2019914935
ISBN: Hardcover   978-1-9845-9193-7
               Softcover   978-1-9845-9192-0
               eBook   978-1-9845-9191-3

Print information available on the last page.

Rev. date: 10/03/2019

To order additional copies of this book, contact:
Xlibris
800-056-3182
www.Xlibrispublishing.co.uk
Orders@Xlibrispublishing.co.uk
799645

I would like to dedicate this book to my wife, Jenn. She was my best friend, my partner, whom I shared all the adventures, trials, and tribulations with for sixty years until she passed away on March of 2015. So with grateful thanks, RIP, my darling. Thank you, Jenn. I will always love you.

Brian XXXXX

From Rookie to Retirement, 1960 to 1990, Warts and All, PC 1538

My Customers Were Never Right

I Do Not Believe It

The Life of Brian and Jenn

CHAPTER ONE

Growing and learning together, facing all the life problems together, raising a family, and holding down jobs in very hard times

My brother Gordon and cousin Bobby play a part on our journey, so I must begin at five years old. My brother was one and a half years older, and my cousin was one year older. I was born into a working-class family in Gateshead, County Durham, in July of 1937. We lived in a downstairs terrace flat, with two bedrooms and a living/dining room, together with a scullery and a bathroom. Cousin Bobby came to live with us at the start of my schooldays.

We all slept in a double bed in the back room. We were together until I was fourteen years old. My mum was Mildred, a very gentle women who was very religious. My dad was a great man to me. Thomas or Tot as he was known. He took me everywhere and taught me many, many things. His family—Grandad, brothers, cousins—all worked in the family businesses. They were coal and coke merchants, and my dad was into haulage contracting.

His four sisters were running a market garden, a taxi business, a fish shop, and a grocery shop, and they were also taking care of housework. Grandad had horses, carts, etc. So they were all involved. Meg was the oldest sister; she got married and immigrated to Australia. The other three—Anne, Ada, and Hilda—remained at home (spinsters). Ada ran the house, and Anne took care of the coal business customers.

Hilda was in the shop selling groceries. Uncle Jack and his sons ran the coal side. There was no TV yet. Public transport were tram cars on rails and buses. There were no mobile phones or PCs. In my street, there were 120 flats, and only two people had landline phones—my dad and his friend at the other end of the street. No one in the street owned a car. Our phone number was 72651. Bobby, Gordon, and I all went to the same school. Bobby was a class higher than me.

Gordon was two classes higher because of the age difference. When I went to school, they had their own clique of friends. We all got together at playtimes and lunchtimes. Altogether, there was quite a gang, approximately thirty. As I was the youngest, they all bullied me, made me run errands, played jokes on me, embarrassed me, and punched and kicked me daily. When Gordon and Bobby saw the bruises, they too abused me for letting the bullies hurt me.

Generally, they took care of me without me knowing. Eventually, the bullies tried to make friends with me. I found this confusing, until I found out that Gordon and Bobby, together with their mates, had found out who they were and beat the crap out of them. We all moved on from infants to juniors and on to senior school at eleven years. We all did our own thing, but the gang kept an eye on me and made sure I was okay. We all played on the football team and cricket team. I enjoyed the swimming team.

I was able to win a Bronze medal and as bronze cross for passing the exams and tests set by the Royal Life Saving Society and was active in the polo team. Before I left school, I think I was eleven stones. My friend Kenny and I went fishing at the bay in Cullercoats seaside resort. It was a small bay with piers on the north and south sides. We were on the south pier. I was casting my line out to the sea, and Ken was behind me casting into the mouth of the bay. We were chatting away and laughing.

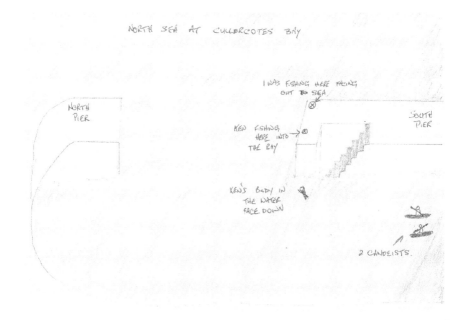

It all went quiet. I could not hear Ken. I looked around, but he was gone. I did not understand. I went to where he had been, and I saw him face down, floating out to sea. I panicked. I shouted at some canoeists for help. I ran along the pier to tell some blokes fishing to call an ambulance. I ran back and plunged off the pier into the sea. I had Gordon's suit on; I borrowed it without asking. I got to Ken and, with the canoeists' help, got Ken to the bottom of the steps.

The other fisherman helped me get him up on to the pier. He hadn't drowned; he was coughing up water and spluttering. He had a cut on his forehead and had a broken wrist. The paramedics said I had saved him, then they took him to the hospital. A copper lent me some dry trousers and sandals, and I had to get on the train home with all the fishing gear. I went to see Ken before I left. He told me he had stepped backwards to cast his line and fell on to the stairs and into the sea.

He passed out. He had stitches on his head, and his wrist had been set in a cast, but he seemed okay. My teacher Mr Martin, the one who strapped me three days a week, jumped on the bandwagon and wrote to the Royal Humane Society and told them about Ken and I. They issued a life-saving certificate on parchment that said I had saved Ken's life. It was a publicity for the school, and he claimed I learned to swim at school.

I had to go to Tynemouth and be presented this award by the lord mayor. Photos were hung in the school.

Dad (left) teacher (right)

After we left school, I never saw Ken again to this day. I also went to the coal yard and to Ada's house to help with the work. The men were loading and delivering, and I was shovelling coal from the heap into bags for weighing and storage. This continued until I left school at fifteen years. With all the work and exercise at fifteen years, I was now six feet and twelve stones, with no fat on me.

Having gained confidence from Gordon and Bobby, I could take care of myself. When Gordon left school at fifteen years, he was supposed to join the family business, but he ran away from home. He lied about his age and signed on a shell tanker as a cabin boy and went around the world. Bobby returned to his home. So I was on my own at home. My dad taught me most things I know. He had me driving lorries in the yard.

I loaded them from the hoppers then parked them, ready for the drivers when they came in. When I left school, I had a job waiting for me at an agency for Vauxhall cars and Bedford trucks. I was an apprentice mechanic, so I could go to college three days a week and work in the garage the other four. I am getting ahead of myself, so I will go back to being fourteen years old.

At school so I can introduce another friend. I had to attend woodwork classes on a Wednesday. When I got to the class, it was closed, but a notice said classes were being held at a nearby school. So off I went, and when I passed the school's playing fields, the whole school was out and was supporting the football and hockey teams. So I joined the spectators and watched the games. At one point, the hockey team came close to us. So I cheered the girls on.

They were very fast and very good, and in the centre of this bunch, one girl was really tackling hard, twisting and turning and having a great game. She was giving instructions to the other girls. She was the most fantastic girl I had ever seen in my life. She had long legs, narrow hips, and a chest that was forming beautifully. She had a lovely face and beautiful teeth/smile.

When she caught me looking at her, she knocked the ball away, and the team went after it. She was coming towards me, smiling. I was uncomfortable and felt funny inside and was aroused. She said, 'Hello, my name is Jenny. What's yours?'

I stumbled on my words and said, 'Brian.'

She said, 'Meet me at the gate at four o'clock. Bye.' Off she went in her navy knickers and team colours. I felt so stupid and embarrassed because she had spoken to me, and that funny feeling was the biggest erection I have ever had.

I didn't go to school. I went home and tried to talk to Mum. I was so naive. I just asked why this was happening, and she was about to try and explain Sod's law (when someone interrupt and distracts everyone from the subject) when Gordon came in, latched on to bits of conversation, put two and two together, and said, 'Get out of here you dirty little wanker.' And then he chased me to my room. I did not meet Jenny, but I raced to her school every night until I caught her coming out. We became friends, and I preferred her company to the boys.

We went to the pictures a few times, but it was an on–off type of thing until we left school. She got a job as a seamstress at Jacksons Tailoring Factory, and we had to plan our days around weekends. We just spent more and more time together. I was totally besotted with her—unbelievably besotted. The end result of that first meeting was, we got engaged in 1956 and married in 1958. We had Derek in 1959 and the twins in 1962.

CHRISTINE   DEREK   JULIE

A lot happened in those years, and I will be telling you in good time. Jenn and I were married for fifty-seven years, and the rest of the notes were the adventures we shared along the way. We were engaged for three years, and I knew her for another two years before that. So all in all, I shared sixty-two to sixty-three years with her before she passed away in March 2015. I miss her so much always, in every waking second of my life. Jenn was totally different to the company I kept.

She was very quick in assessing people and situations and was capable of reaching solutions long before I did. I loved her sense of humour. She soon sussed I was a virgin and was happy to share that she was too. The factory girls where she worked explained all aspects of sex to her, and she educated me. We understood it but had no experience in putting it into practice. So we were content with kisses and cuddles and were still virgins when we got engaged at seventeen years.

Other things were going on at work for me. Alan, my mentor and tutor mechanic, had, unknown to me, entered my name for a training course at Vauxhall Motors in Luton for training on diesel engines. Only a few makes of lorries had diesel engines. Certainly, no cars had them at that time. Vauxhall Motors sent me to a plant which produced Perkins diesel engines, where I learned all about these engines and how to adjust, tune, and repair them.

At the end of the course, I passed the practical tests and oral exams, which made me feel good, because my dad would be proud of me. I was given a certificate that said I had passed, which I still have today.

Me (left holding spanner)

I found learning pretty easy and seemed to grasp what we were taught quickly. It surprised me because I was the youngest trainee allowed on the course. When we came home, three of us brought brand-new cars back to the agency in Newcastle.

I hadn't seen Jenn, but because my dad had a phone, he let me reverse the charges so I could speak to her every day. I really missed her being away. When I was by myself, I cried. I was so pleased to be back with her. This crying was an emotion I had only known through pain. So much for being a very tough bully. Jenn's home life was very different to mine. Her dad was an alcoholic tyrant. There were five more siblings—two brothers (Colin and Joe) and three sisters (Muriel, Margaret, and Ann). The only way I was allowed into the house at first was to pretend I was Joe's friend—at least that got me into the house—but alcoholic or not, he quickly worked out it was Jenn I came to see. Eventually, he got used to the idea. When he was sober, he was okay, but when drunk, he was a wife beater, something I had not known about until I saw the black eyes of Jenn's mum. It soon became apparent that he hit all the kids as well.

There had been occasions where Jenn had stood up to him. He backed down when he was sober, but when drunk, he had hit her. So like all bullies, he was really a coward. The age he lived in was ancient, and he still believed I should ask for Jenn's hand in marriage. He was tyrannical enough to believe it. He did not like me, but he tolerated me. He was five feet, four inches, and I was six feet, so he had a little man's chip on his shoulders. We became wary of each other. Jenn and I got engaged, and he made it known that he wanted me to ask for Jenn's hand.

I called at Jenn's, and he was upstairs decorating. The family was excited because it was a good time to ask him, so I went upstairs to see him. He was at the top of the stepladder.

I said, 'Can I speak to you?'

He said, 'Yes, come in.' He put down the paintbrush, and he sat on top of the steps, waiting and grinning like a Cheshire cat. He said, 'Okay, go on then.'

So I got the second set of steps and sat on the top step, which meant he was looking up at me instead of down. This unnerved him, and he was becoming agitated. So I said, 'Jenn and I are engaged, and we have set a date. The marriage will be on the first of March. I am not going to ask your permission, and I will tell you, if I hear one word out of place from you and if you lift your hands to Jenn or any other member of the family, I will bar you from the wedding completely. Don't answer me. Just think about what I have said.' I walked out and left him.

Downstairs, Jenn asked me. 'Was everything okay?'

I said, 'Yes, it's fine. Your dad is well pleased.'

Jenn and I went to the pictures, and I told her what I had said. She was worried about him retaliating when he gets drunk. I said, 'I don't think that will happen.'

The wedding came, and he gave Jenn away. But as he walked her down the aisle, she told him, 'When you let go of my arm, I will never allow you to touch me again.' It was a lovely wedding, and everyone enjoyed it. I now had a motorbike, and we went out more often with the gang.

All the girls liked Jenn, and we all got on very well. When I was away from Jenn, I was still a bully and had an extreme temper. My dad said my violence was only a short-term answer. That if I got into trouble, I should always walk away no matter what, always try to walk away. But if that was not possible, then to save being hurt, I defended myself by getting in first and physically stop it in the first two minutes.

I incapacitated whomever was picking on me. I have always tried to follow dad's advice, where possible, to walk away. One guy was always having a go at me at work. He would thump my arms so hard they would go numb. He was in his late twenties. I was seventeen years. He would knee me in the legs from the side so hard that sometimes I would fall, and my legs would be dead for ages. I told the fitter I was an apprentice to. He, Alan, was an ex-marine commando.

In his late thirties, he was very big—six feet three, muscular and strong, built like a brick outhouse. I told him this treatment had been going on a long time since I started work at fifteen. He talked to me and asked me not to say or do anything, and he would have words with Nick. We worked as usual, and I came into contact with Nick. He just swore and cursed me for being a baby and getting Alan to sort him out. I just walked away, embarrassed and fuming.

During my time spent working with Alan, a couple of minor accidents happened. The first was when Alan wore a metal ring on his right hand's third finger. He was reaching into a lorry engine bay lorry behind the generator, and his ring made contact with live terminals and became white hot instantly. Alan pulled out his hand and asked me to open a vice on the workbench. He gripped the ring in the jaws of the vice and told me to get a hacksaw and cut the ring through, which I did. He then opened the ring and removed his hand. He checked the wound, and the skin where the ring had been was burnt to the bone, and the remaining skin had been cauterised. He and I went to see the first aider. She was also the canteen manager. She was also very squeamish, and Alan ended up cleaning and dressing the wound himself. He also filled in the workbook and recorded the incident. One other incident much later—his hand had healed—was when we were working underneath the rear end of a seven-ton truck. There was plenty of room, and we were trying to loosen u bolt nuts in order to remove the springs, so we unbolted the nuts in order to remove the rear springs. I had previously covered the nuts with penetrating oil. We were able to sit on the floor and put a very large spanner on to the nuts. This spanner was three feet long and could not budge the nuts even with our feet braced up on the rear axle. Alan got a piece of piping and extended the spanner by two feet. He sat with his bum on the floor and his feet on the rear axle to get more purchase on the spanner. The nut gave way with an almighty crack, and Alan fell backwards as the spanner had hit him across his left eye. He had a gash from the middle of his face through his left eyebrow and down to his cheekbone. It was wide open and needed stitches. He sent me to tell the nurse in the canteen to be ready for him. He went to the washing room and cleaned up most of the blood, and when he got back to the nurse, she could not help as she was queasy again. He sat down and asked me to help him by getting the first-aid equipment. We set up a portable mirror on a table, and while I held the padding on the wound, he threaded a needle and suture. When he was ready, he began to stitch the wound. It was very neat and tidy, and very little blood could escape from the wound. The paramedics arrived and examined Alan. He refused their help, and he took the next couple of days off after completing the accident report book.

In the workshop, there was a wooden structure which led to a place where we could go to collect spare parts from the stores upstairs without going to the main shop and front sales counter. There was a serving hatch at floor level to the stores but chest high to those collecting parts. I was waiting in there for the storeman to bring my spares. Nick came in and saw me.

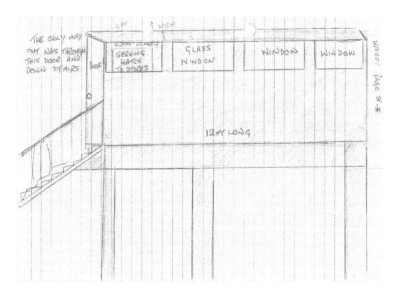

He started pushing me back and punching me. I pushed back and saw the storeman put my parts in a box for me to pick up. He shouted at Nick, telling him to pack it in and keep the noise down. Nick said, 'Come and get your bits then.' I tried to reach into the hatch. Nick punched me in the side so hard I fell sideways, and he came at me again. I realised I had two four-foot-long steel brake cables kept together by a steel plate in my hand.

THE CABLES WERE SUPPLIED IN PAIRS AND WERE HELD TOGETHER WITH TWO PIECES OF STEEL PLATE. THE CABLES WOULD HAVE BEEN COILED UP TO SAVE SPACE.

4FT LONG CABLES. MADE OF STEEL WIRE.

As I struggled to get up, the cables uncoiled, and to protect myself from Nick, I swung the cables at him. They were like steel whips. By now I was shaking. He would not let me out. I felt the red mist come down. I kicked at him to drive him back. I lashed him and lashed him. He was screaming, then the storeman was screaming. I became very calm, and all I could hear was silence. As I continued to lash Nick, blood was everywhere.

Nick was on the floor, his body on the floor and his back against the door, stopping it from opening. I kept on lashing and beating him with the cables. I was covered in blood. My hearing came back. The screaming was horrendous. The door burst open. Alan came in and pushed me to the back wall, and I gave him the cables. He told me to go and get washed and then go to the canteen and wait for him.

The end result was that Nick was taken to the hospital and put in intensive care. He was there for some time. He had to have skin grafts and operations, which were going to be a long job. I was sent home and suspended for three days, until they decided what to do with me, either to sack me or not. Alan saved the day, and all blame was put on Nick. The ambulance people told the police, and they came to interview me and take statements.

They said they would come back when everyone had been interviewed. In the meantime, my uncle said I could go with him for a few days. He was a waiter on the express train from London to Edinburgh. But he also did catering on ships which were going out on trials before being taken over by the owners. So I went out as a cabin boy to help out in the galley. We sailed from Swan Hunters yard and out to sea at Tynemouth.

About eight to nine miles downriver, we went up and down the coast about ten mile offshore. The weather changed to gale force, and I began to be seasick. It was awful. I have never been seasick before. They would not launch a small boat to take me ashore because there was only skeleton staff on board. The weather got worse, and the medics on board took care of me. It was so bad the tanker could not get back into the River Tyne.

So I was stuck out at sea for three weeks instead of three days. I was so ill. I thought I would die and be buried at sea. I thought I would never see Jenn or Mum/Dad again. We eventually came ashore, and I went home to bed. My mum took care of me. This was the first time in my life my mum talked about her church and religion. She belonged to the First Church of Christ, Scientist, which originated in America and established by Mary Baker Eddy.

She talked about the healing power of Jesus and how some ordinary people could have these powers. I wasn't even half listening; I was feeling so ill and weak. I could hear her talking, but it seemed so far away. The next day, she gave me some breakfast and asked if I had listened yesterday. She also told me that by dinner time, Jenn would be here, and I had better get up and cleaned before she came. I felt awful and did not want to be bothered.

But Mum pulled my blankets off me and got me up. Strangely, I did not feel so bad. I had a bath, and by eleven o'clock, I was dressed and waiting. Jenn came, and we talked and cuddled all afternoon. She was as amazed as I was about my recovery. We went to the pictures after tea. The next day, I was up early and out with my dad, like I had never been sick at all. I have never been seasick since. I returned to work, and all was well.

Alan told me about police interviews and meetings with the management who all decided that I acted in self-defence and that no further action would be taken. The police came to see me at home and gave us the news officially. No further was action to be taken. The officer told me Nick was out of intensive care and having skin grafts. He would not be at work for a long time. He also asked if I had ever thought about joining the police force.

I said I had not given it any thought because I was an apprentice and deferred from the army until 1958. Then I would be conscripted for two years. The officer said that would be good. After the army, I would be twenty-three and could start a career, which would allow me to retire after twenty-five years. By then, I would be forty-eight and retired with a pension. After he left, I talked about this with Mum and Dad. My dad wanted me in the haulage business with him.

But he said it was my life, to think about it. I talked to Jenn about it, and she said it sounded okay. If I wanted a career, she said to go for it. But events took a different turn. My dad became ill, and I had a bad accident on my motorbike. It happened on my way to work on a Friday morning. I received injuries which incapacitated me for a long time. My right leg was fractured in seven places below the knee, my ankle joint had been pushed out through my boot, and my leg mangled.

I needed surgery. I was taken to Newcastle infirmary and put on the accident ward. It was full of people with injuries, all moaning and wailing. Some were with arms or legs missing. It was an awful place for a seventeen-year-old to be. I had managed to get a nurse to phone Mum. Mum and Aunt Margaret turned up to see me. I could feel no pain. The doctors had placed my broken leg into a half-cast mould to get it rested, and nothing more was to be done over the weekend until all swelling had subsided.

There was a complication. They injected my good leg with penicillin and found I was allergic to it. My leg swelled up badly; it was twice the size of the other one. So they had to get that right before surgery on Monday. My mum came on Saturday and Sunday to visit. We talked and talked about what doctors had said. Mum said, 'Please be quiet and listen carefully to me.' She went on and said that the doctors and nurses were all given training and teaching to heal people.

'They have one purpose—to make you well. And they will, and I will help them to help you. I have decided you are coming home a week next Friday. You will have surgery on Monday and recuperate until we go home on Friday. The operation will be a success. Your leg will not be three inches shorter, and it will face forward like it always has been. There will be no after-effects. All will heal naturally.'

The weekend passed. My swollen left leg was normal size again. My right leg was aching. Monday came. Mum came into the ward early. She sat with me, and her hand was resting on my broken leg. She reminded me of the power of a healing mind. They took me to surgery. I felt very calm and quiet; my legs felt normal. The surgeons surrounded the table, and they lifted me on to it. They were all in masks and gloves.

One placed a needle in the back of my hand and asked me to count backwards. I know now it was the anaesthetist. I counted backwards and drifted off into oblivion.

First out-of-body experience

Suddenly, I could hear the team talking to each other. I could see them all from about two feet above their heads. I watched them cut my leg open wide and lift the broken bones into place. They put my ankle back together, and I watched everything. It seemed to go very quickly, but it took 2.5 hours. They put silver screws into a plate in my ankle and were pleased it was going well. They were nearly done. I heard the leading surgeon thank his team and dismiss them one at a time.

They left, until two remained—the head surgeon and the anaesthetist. The surgeon said, 'I am closing now.' And he put a couple more stitches in the wound. He said, 'That's it. I am done. Did you see the match on Saturday?' At that point, I felt myself roll on to my back and lower myself into my body. When I woke up again, I was in a recovery room, and Mum was there waiting for me to come around.

Everyone else had left the room. She held my hand and said, 'Don't worry. Everything is fine, like I told you it would be.' In the next few days, she and Jenn spent a lot of time together. Mum told me to make sure I would take care of Jenn, and she would look after me. I later came to believe my mother had helped the doctors, and she had performed a miracle. I left the hospital on Friday and went home with Mum.

I had a plaster cast up to my hip. It took six months and two more casts before the hospital let me go. In all, I was off work for a year. In that time, my dad had taken ill and was bedridden. Jenn and I got engaged, and I sold my motorbike to buy an engagement ring. A fortune teller gypsy, Rose Lee, read Jenn's fortune and told her that she would have three children but only two pregnancies and that, at a later stage, she would live abroad for a long time.

The family split the businesses between them. Older cousins Tom and Richard took over the coal yard. Hilda and Annie kept one shop. The market garden, fish shop, and taxi businesses were all sold. My dad was left with one lorry. He became so ill he had to sell it. I was with him when the buyer took it away. I saw him cry and realised he was not going to get better. Dad died just before my eighteenth birthday in 1955. Jenn and I talked about what we would do in the future now.

I said I did not want to be a fitter any more. She obviously talked with Mum. She asked me how I felt about having a family and planning a future for us. Firstly, we were still virgins. Talking about having kids and planning a family, Jenn suggested we could marry before I went in the army. We were twenty years old and still virgins on our wedding day. We were married on 1 March 1958 and had only until December to get organised.

Jenn stayed at her mother's when I left in December '58. She managed to get a one-room flat, and we furnished and decorated it. Jenn was pregnant and due in Dec of '59. I got compassionate leave. Derek was born on 10 December '59. This was the beginning of a fabulous time for us. We put into practice what the factory girls had told Jenn, and we fumbled and bungled our way through.

We must have got it right since Jenn got pregnant. All this was great. We learned as we went. The bonus for me was, Jenn turned into a nymphomaniac. She turned into my martini girl at any time, anywhere, anyhow. It got better, and it lasted all our lives. That's enough. Some things are really private and will remain that way forever. Jenn was coming home from the hospital just before Xmas, so I thought I would make the flat warm and kept an open fire going day and night.

She came home on Xmas eve, and all was well. The baby was great and smiled all the time. On Xmas Day, we had visitors bringing gifts and presents for the baby. After 4 p.m. we were quiet, and the visitors were all gone. I had just put the baby in bed in the other room. When I came back into the living room, Jenn said she could see smoke coming from the tiles on the fireplace. I checked and could see the smoke, so I took a piece of fireplace wood to one side.

That let the oxygen in, and the whole fireplace burst into flames. I sent Jenn to get the landlord from downstairs. They were back in a flash. I asked Jenn to take the baby and all she needed to her mum's and to call the fire service. The landlord was shouting at us and going mad. Jenn left, and the fire brigade arrived. They moved all our furniture to the back of the room and covered it with carpet.

They brought a hose and started damping down the fireplace. The landlord was shouting and arguing with them. Two of them took him out of the room and told him to stay downstairs. One of the firemen I became very friendly with told me, 'You won't be able to stay here with the baby when we are finished.' Then he took a hammer and broke out the whole fireplace and lifted the floorboards.

The landlord had put concrete in between the floor joists, which had heated up and took fire. A whole section of the ceiling collapsed into the landlord's room. He was going crazy. The firemen went on to the roof and put a hose down the chimney. It washed all the soot into the landlord's room. He went even crazier. The young fireman called Roy and I had a good laugh, and he said I might as well go.

He would lock up my rooms and leave the key on the picture rail. So I went and found Jenn. We took the baby to my mum's and stayed there. So that was goodbye to our first home. Within a few days, a house opposite her mum's came up for rent. We took it and moved in. What we salvaged from the first house helped a lot. My leave finished, and I returned to my unit. Postings came up for twenty-nine men— fourteen to Hong Kong, fourteen to Singapore, and one to Shropshire. I had access to the office and signed for Shropshire. Everyone just accepted it. After a short while, I took leave, went home, and bought a twelve-seater Dormobile and started a bus service for every weekend from Shropshire to Newcastle and back. It also meant a means of extra income for Jenn. Time passed, and I was discharged, but I had to remain on reserve for six years.

I finished two wasted years in December '60 and temporarily went back to work in the garage. Jenn persuaded me to pack it in and start a career. I applied, passed the entrance exam, and joined the Gateshead County Borough Police. I was a probationary officer for two years, which meant I could be dismissed without being given a reason. If I managed the two years, I would be accepted as a regular officer.

I had to go to a training college for three months with an exam at the end of each month. Then there would be a passing out parade followed by a dance if successful in passing the exams. It was very military, and uniform had to be worn at all times. There were two other recruits from Gateshead—one from Durham and the other was my friendly fireman Roy. He left the fire service and joined the police.

We became friends and spent all spare time together. He had an old car, so my transport problem was solved. I had sold my Dormobile. We got home on a Friday night and back on a Sunday night; otherwise, we would not be on the campus on time. After a couple of weeks, we got bored, so we left camp via the cookhouse window at ground level and left it unlocked for our return. We visited the local haunts and got talking to people, so we soon found our way about.

There were recruits from many forces at the college. The dining hall sat 300 when full, including the top table where all the brass—commandant, chief superintendent, etc.—sat. Most of the recruits had never been away from home and could not handle the regimental side of training, to instil discipline and compliance to rules and regulations. When you entered the hall for a meal, you were not allowed to sit until the duty officer on the top table sat.

You had to stand behind your chair and wait. I had just spent two years of this pomp and ceremony in the army with middle-rank officers screaming orders at us. It didn't take long to work out that if we (Roy and I) sat close to the door, we could not be seen from the top table because of the surrounding structures holding up the ceiling. So we adopted this area and just sat when we entered without waiting for the duty officer.

Other students saw us sitting and followed suit. This caused chaos with everyone, and lectures came every mealtime on etiquette, which Roy and I ignored. Word went around, and we were branded troublemakers, to be watched carefully as we set a bad example to younger recruits. By the end of the second month, we had been hauled into the commandant's office several times and told off for conduct unbecoming to officers.

We continued our trips into town and were hauled up again in front of the duty officer. He was reluctant to put us in front of the commandant because we were nearly finished the course. So we were warned once again. Roy said he had some business to take care of in town, and I did not see him for a few evenings. He was very secretive about his outings, but I suspected whatever it was, it would mean trouble, and he kept me out of it.

Another recruit from Yorkshire carried the same collar numbers as Roy, and he had been goading Roy most of the time we had been there. At 4 p.m., I was on my way walking from the classroom block to the dining hall. As I was getting near the hall, the Yorkshire lad hurried past me and caught up to Roy. He pushed Roy, and an argument turned into a fight. I started to run and got to them outside the windows of the hall.

Roy hit this guy so hard he lifted him off his feet and he crashed through the window into the dining hall behind the top table. I grabbed Roy and dragged him with me. We were out of sight of the windows and were behind the next building. We decided to brazen it out and quietly go to dinner. Our regular seats were vacant, so we sat down. Everyone by now was seated, but confusion reigned around the top table.

The guy Roy hit was being trolleyed out, and people were sweeping up broken glass. Roy and I finished our meal and returned to the dormitory. The next morning, we were sent for and questioned about the events. We kept quiet and denied all knowledge of what had happened. The commandant tore strips off us and said if he could have proved we were involved, he would have sent us home. But as a punishment, our wives were not allowed at the dance at the end of the course, and we would be given the jobs of ushers to guests turning up.

Roy went quietly, fuming and mad. His wife had bought a new outfit. We decided not to tell our wives and take a chance we would not be thrown out. Roy went into town and had some invitation cards printed for this dance at the police training college, and he dished them all out to the local prostitutes who jumped at the chance of attending the dance which was on a Thursday. And we would all be going home on Friday of the next week.

Roy told me he had some gear to take home this week—tomorrow. We picked up the gear and went home. The dance was okay. Jenn and Roy's wife came and enjoyed the night until about eightish, when a bus turned up with all the working girls coming for free booze and nosh. They danced with everyone who was free. The officers' wives complained, and the whole thing turned into shambles.

Roy and I took our wives downtown and had a meal off camp. The wives went home, and Roy and I went back to the college. Not much work got done Friday, and we were allowed off camp early. We took Roy's car and went around a few country lanes. He pulled into a driveway, and we loaded the car with forty Xmas trees all tied up and ready to pack. He said he had bought them.

He dropped me at home and said he would pick me up in the morning. He did, and we went to South Shields market, where his uncle had a stall. All trees were sold before dinner, so he dropped me at home Saturday afternoon. On Sunday, we were all back on campus, and it was quiet. At breakfast, the senior ranks on the top table said, 'There would be an enquiry going on. Apparently, the commandant had been away on the weekend and, on his return, found someone had cut down and taken all his Xmas trees.'

I nearly choked on my tea. It all went down the wrong way. I did not dare look at Roy. Sure enough, we were called into the office for interviews about the damn trees. The commandant said if we had not been due to leave on Friday, he would have us both sacked. Roy protested and argued with him until he ordered us out of his office. 'You two won't last five minutes as police officers on the street. I shall be talking to your chief constable about you pair.' Friday came, and we left. I never heard anything more about the college.

Alfred Street was our second home. Jenn had settled in and made it nice. So now we were probationers at Gateshead. We were living opposite Jenn's mum, so we always had lots of company. With Margaret, Ann, Joe, Colin, and Jenn's mum, there was always someone visiting.

I was reporting to the main police station in Gateshead town centre, getting used to being with the public and their reaction to seeing me in uniform. I was assigned to a tutor constable. His name was Cecil Wright. I crossed paths and swords with him many times in the past as a teenager. He once chased me, and as I was near home, I ran to my back door, next to which was a coal hatch.

I could jump to reach the top of the wall and vault over to lie flat on the coalhouse roof. Cecil burst through our back door on his bike, went down two steps, and fell off. My dad was also leaving the house at this time; he came up the yard and tried to help Cecil get up. Unfortunately, their combined weight broke the manhole cover they were standing on, and my dad dropped down six to seven feet into the shaft leading to the main drains.

My dad could see me on the roof, and he had time to signal me to go before Cecil helped him out. I ran and went to Aunty Hilda's for an hour. Luckily, my dad landed on his feet and was not hurt. Cecil apparently went about his duty elsewhere. Cecil and I were to be together for one month until he had shown me the boundaries of each beat. He held no grudges against me. We had a good month. He taught me so much in such a short time.

I saw a completely different side to him. There were so many rules and regulations to learn about each beat, and we had to make pocketbook entries every fifteen minutes to show where we were and note about any occurrence that we dealt with. Cecil is the only officer I have seen use old English copperplate writing in his pocketbook. It was a work of art, so lovely. The town was divided into twenty-four beats. Even numbers carried night shifts; odd numbers were 6 p.m.–2 a.m. After which the night shift was responsible for both beats until the early-shift men arrived.

There were five shifts on a rota system. Even numbers were early, 6 a.m.–2 p.m.; late, 2 p.m.–10 p.m.; and nights, 10 p.m.–6 a.m. Odd numbers were middle days, 8.30 a.m.–4.30 p.m. so that officers could cover school crossing patrols. The other shift was half nights, 6 p.m.–2 a.m., to overlap lates and nights at the busy times between 10.30 drinking time and 10.40 pub closing time. People were not allowed to loiter outside pubs, and the streets had to be clear by 11.30.

If they were not, the PC could be disciplined by a visiting sergeant or inspector. That could mean a fine for the beat PC or a reprimand for a probationer officer. Each beat was equipped with a police box, a blue flashing light on top, and emergency phones for the public. They were a good size, 12-12 as about the normal. Inside were benches, chairs, an electric fire, and an electric kettle. Officers could spend their break time, 3/4 hour, to have tea and sandwiches.

Also, there were files on all felons and villains living on the patch, which we had to memorise and take notes if they were seen, who they were with, and if there were any vehicles in their possession.

They also had lists of keyholders for shops, pubs, dance halls, pictures, and any important buildings. As a probie, we had to read them all on each beat. It was also expected that each PC would learn where doctors, nurses, and midwives lived and where you could get timber and joiners to board up property that was damaged (shop windows) and the like.

If HQ wanted to contact you and you were away from the box 'Tardis', they would leave on the blue light flashing, and members of the public would inform PCs they were wanted on the phone. During the day shift, all PCs would walk the beat on the outside of the pavement so they could be seen at a distance. The pace would be 2.5 miles per hour. On nights and half nights, PCs would walk close to shop windows and doors and check all doors to premises were locked and would wear night-duty uniform—no shiny buttons and whistle chains, black buttons, and badges—so as not to be seen in the darkness.

It was fairly regimented, like a lot of old regulations were outdated. PCs could not have a moustache or beard or get married without the chief constable's consent. PCs could not be in any debt or gamble. PCs' wives could not have a job, business, etc. And for a PC, especially a probationer, to be off his beat and get caught was a sacking offence, unless you were dealing with an emergency.

There were dozens of little bylaws to learn. It was a very busy month. Cecil, my tutor, would offer advice on every incident we attended, most of his advice I carried with me through my service for years. Like never close the door to the Tardis if there was a female inside to prevent any allegations being made. Always stand near the open door so you could be seen by passersby. Even to the point of asking a member of the public to stand in the box with you until transport arrived. If they were under arrest,

It was very important to protect yourself. *Never ever trust anyone.* When I came to beat 14, I read the felons' files, and looking at the pictures, I recognised my cousin Bobby and read his file. I had not seen him for a few years. He had turned to crime around eighteen years old. He had been arrested and done time in prison. He was listed as extremely violent to officers, and PCs should have backup before making an arrest.

I could not believe what I was reading. Cecil knew him personally and confirmed the reports. I said nothing to any other officer. I told Jenn, and she said to make contact with him off duty and find out for myself. During the month, I met most of the other officers and seemed to get on quite well with them. The month ended, and I was to be on my own from here on. The rota did not apply to probationers; we were put on any vacant beat to cover. After six months, I was posted on the bottom of the town, a really bad area called the Teams.

This particular patch was full of villains, and a gang of about fifteen yobs were ruling the area, daily terrorising the shopkeepers and public. A posting lasting three months or thirteen weeks and then you were moved on to another beat. It was my job to sort out the gang. I spoke to Cecil, and he told me to learn their first names or nicknames and make sure I could recognise them by the photos and associates.

If I saw them, I was to speak to them and use their first names as though I had known them for years, ask them if they were okay, and keeping their noses clean. They asked if I was new or transferred in. They also asked my name. Some of them knew my brother, and all of them knew my cousin Bobby. Word of who I was went around very quickly, and respect was born between us over a period of six to nine months. I was kept on that posting for two years.

I had run-ins with them all as individuals. I arrested four to five over that time, and things were building up to a bust-up. A younger PC than me asked if I would do him a favour and swap shifts on Saturday. He would do my six to two, and I would do his eight thirty to four thirty. He had some family do on during the day. Every day, at some point, a sergeant and a duty inspector would visit to make sure I was doing my job and my notebook kept up to date.

When the sergeant came on Sunday night, he told me the young PC had taken a bad beating at the hands of the gang. I had also contacted Bobby, and he and I had a long talk. I told him I thought some of the gang were his boys in the words of villains. He just said, 'Leave it to me.' He and his henchmen used a nightclub in Chester-le-Street ten miles out of town. As it happened, Jenn and I used the same club when shifts allowed.

Jenn and I went one night later, and we saw Bobby and his cronies at one big table. None of them spoke, and we were shown to a table away from them. A waitress came and gave Jenn a bottle of wine and said it was from the big table. When I looked around, Bobby and everyone else had gone. There was a note with the bottle, saying, 'Enjoy your night. Bobby.' On the back of the note were two names—Ginger and Blackie. These two were the main leaders of the mob. Blackie was the top man, and Ginger was the muscle.

I watched both of them for a few weeks and noted their habits and movements. Some methods I adopted were not in the code of ethics, so I adopted the ways by any means act, to get results. A few nights later, I saw Ginger. He was on the rear platform of a double-decker bus; he was singing and shouting at the passengers and appeared drunk. On all bus stop posts, there were steel rubbish bins with a removable liner. As the bus passed me, Ginger got tangled up with the bin liner and fell into the road.

The bus carried on, and I arrested Ginger for being drunk and disorderly and also charged him with criminal damage to the rubbish bin. I took him to the police box and dressed a wound on his face, then I called an ambulance, and the paramedics sorted out his injuries. I escorted him to the cell block at the police station. I did have a long chat with him, and we discussed his future if he was to continue his lifestyle. He was off work for some time.

Blackie, I observed, had a girlfriend, and he would use the deep pawnshop doorway for a kiss and cuddle before the girlfriend headed home. He would stand and wait until she was nearly out of sight before he would go the opposite way home. I watched him one night and decided to have words with him when his girlfriend left. I ran across to the doorway and grabbed him, and a struggle ensued.

Somehow, the glass in the shop door was broken. This caused the alarms to go off and the lights to come on. I knew the alarm for this shop was connected to HQ, and officers would be coming. All I had to do was hang on to Blackie. The cavalry arrived; Blackie was arrested and went to the hospital to be looked at and patched up. Blackie was charged with burglary and assault on me. Eventually, he went to court and was given a custodial sentence.

While I was posted on the Teams' beat, I was called to deal with a domestic row. It was 11 p.m., and I was on night shift. Another officer was on 6 p.m. until 2 a.m., so we both went together. When we got to the house, a woman said she lived there with her boyfriend who was drunk and could not cope with the noise of the crying kids.

The other PC had a lot more experience than I, so he took charge and asked the lady questions like 'What is the boyfriend's name?' and 'Is he really drunk?' She said, 'He's in the living room listening to the records and watching TV.' I never heard what his name was.

We entered the living room. When the boyfriend saw us, he leapt out of his chair, and he launched a beer bottle at us, which hit the wall about head height to my left. It smashed to pieces. He began ranting and swearing and telling us what he would do if we did not get out. Scotty, my police partner, stood his ground and asked where the kids were. By the body language and stance, the boyfriend was ready to do battle.

He muttered, 'In the bloody bin.' Scotty asked me to check, and when I hesitated, he said, 'Just go! The kids are the priority. I can chat with our friend.'

I went to the rear yard and checked the bin. I lifted the lid, and *wow*, there were two babies looking at me. They were very clean and well wrapped up. They reminded me of my own twins who were about the same age and size. I picked them up and carried them back through the house and out to the mother, who checked them over and put them into a pram. She was happy and said, 'I will go to my mother's until tomorrow.' I went back indoors, and Scotty had this six-foot-two-inch drunken sailor in cuffs. He was still shouting threats at us. He was taken to HQ and put in a cell. My involvement ended there, and I returned to my beat.

At the end of the cell block passage were two doors. One led to the charge room and station offices. The other door, which was always locked, led to a walkway above the coal and coke storage rooms and out to the rear yard door. The walkway had trap doors above each room, so the deliveries could be made into the storage areas.

When my sergeant came to visit me on my next shift, he questioned me at length about the domestic row and, in particular, what happened at the cell block. Apparently, the prisoner had assaulted Scotty when he tried to interview him the next day, and Scotty had chased him along the cell block passage through the door on to the walkways. The guy had fallen about ten feet into the storage area and had broken both legs, the femur bones in both legs. He was stretchered out and taken to the hospital. He was in plaster for months. In all the times I worked at HQ, I had never seen the back door open. I saw Scotty regularly. He had never mentioned the guy assaulting him or trying to escape. The good news was, the babies were fine, none the worse for the ordeal. A couple of weeks later, I was posted to the High Street beat in the town centre. I think Bobby warned off any remaining gang members, and for the first time in years, peace rained on the Teams' area beats. The High Street was a very busy time on Friday, Saturday, and Sunday. We worked in threes to a section. The High Street was then part of the A1 running from south to the Tyne Bridge.

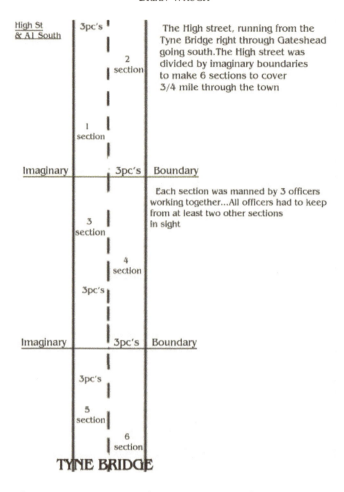

High St
& A1 South   3pc's

2
section

1
section

Imaginary   3pc's   Boundary

3
section

4
section

3pc's

Imaginary   3pc's   Boundary

3pc's

5
section

6
section

TYNE BRIDGE

The High street, running from the
Tyne Bridge right through Gateshead
going south.The High street was
divided by imaginary boundaries
to make 6 sections to cover
3/4 mile through the town

Each section was manned by 3 officers
working together...All officers had to keep
from at least two other sections
in sight

The High Street was over three quarters of a mile long, and it
contained forty-nine pubs, three picture houses, two dance halls,
and seven betting shops. So by 11 p.m., all the pubs were closed, and
customers on the street were looking for taxis, buses, etc. The picture
house goers would be mingling with the crowd.

Most of the crowd would have had a good drink and be worse for
wear. So arguments and fighting were the norm. On each section,
I had to keep at least two other sections in sight at all times when
possible. It just seemed the fighting never ended. Several times in two
years, I was admitted to the hospital with injuries. So were all the other
officers. It was par for the course. Beat men were backed up by traffic
drivers, and prison vans also patrolled the area.

When I joined, I fully believed I wanted to help people whenever possible, but because of so much violence, I was beginning to give up that notion. Before my posting, Jenn was pregnant again, and she gave birth to twins—Christine and Julie—in 1962. The powers that be, the bosses, decided to keep me on the High Street. I was there for two years. I volunteered to work nights so I could help Jenn with the twins during the day.

My bosses allowed me to take my refreshments at home, so I could feed the twins between 1.30 a.m. and 2.15 a.m. If I could not get home, the switchboard girls would direct another officer to my home, and they would take their break and feed the twins. Everyone helped with the twins. Several things happened at home in Alfred Street. Once, I was at home off duty, and my mum was visiting.

She was in the front room with Derek. He was playing with toys. Derek picked up a picnic blanket and put it over his head. He was singing and spinning around. I came in and saw the danger of him spinning towards the fireplace. There was a fairly big fire on, but the fireguard was in place. I told Derek to stop spinning, but his heel hit the hearth. Not aware of the danger, he tried to grab something to stop him from spinning and falling.

I saw his right hand go between the top and middle bars of the fire, and he grabbed on to it. It was glowing between white- and red-hot. I saw and smelt the flesh on his burning hand. My mum was nearest to him, and she also sensed what was happening. She got to Derek first. He was screaming. She grabbed him and spoke quietly to him, keeping the blanket over his head. She told him, 'We are going to play a new game called waterfalls.'

Derek became quiet. Mum told me to get out of the way and that she had control of the situation. She had scooped Derek up in her arms and gone into the kitchen. She sat Derek on the side of the sink. Whilst talking to him all the time, she made sure he had the blanket still over his head. While she explained about the game, she turned on the cold tap and said, 'We are under the waterfall.' Then she ran the water down his arm gently.

Derek was wriggling a bit, but then he sat still and listened. When Mum told him she was going to hold his hand in hers like a sandwich and that they were under the waterfall together and the game was nearly over because Dad wanted to play as well. She held his hand gently in hers and told Derek, 'In a little while, we would be able to go back in the living room and play different games.'

I made sure the twins were okay. They were asleep. I put the fireguard back in place. Mum said, 'We are nearly done. Do you want to join in now? You can take the blanket off Derek's head.' Which I did, and then Mum said, 'Come to this side and hold Derek's hand. Do not be worried. All is well.' I expected to see mutilation after seeing his hand burning on the fire bars. I took his hand and looked at both sides. There were no signs of any burns or damage.

I was breaking down and confused. I went into the other room and cried. I was so confused and upset; I didn't know what to do next. Mum came in with Derek and started playing games without the blanket this time. Mum said, 'Do not doubt what you saw, because I saw it happen as well, and *never doubt the power of healing hands.*' I wanted to go to the doctor's, but Mum assured me it was not necessary.

'There is nothing else for a doctor to do or see, and he won't be pleased at you wasting his time.' Jenn came in, and I told her what had happened and what Mum had done. She was very calm and asked Grandma, 'Are you all right? You've had a busy time. Can I see Derek's hands?'

Derek came to Jenn and showed her his hand and said, 'We played waterfalls in the kitchen—Grandma, Dad, and me.'

Jenn said, 'Well, you look okay. Can you help me now with the shopping?' They both went into the kitchen.

Life went on as usual. My mum talked to me about healing, church, and God. So I accepted there had been a tragedy with injuries all cleared up by a miracle from God through the power of healing hands.

I still believe that day to this day. A few days later, we were at the doctor's with the twins, and Jenn asked him to check Derek's right hand, which he did and said, 'I can't find anything wrong. Has he fallen on it? Every bone is okay. There is no swelling or discolouration. It's fine, and the twins are fine. Also, don't worry, children get lots of bumps and knocks, and they are okay.'

This next incident happened when we were living at Alfred Street, our second home. I accept all kids are prone to it. The next thing I want to mention is the special connection, telepathy, that exists between twins. When one gets hurt, the other twin feels the pain. With my twins, it was noticeable all through early schools when all kids were open to the usual ailments, like measles, whooping cough, scarlatina or scarlet fever, mumps, and so on. Whatever it was, one twin showed all the symptoms and recovered in two or three days, while the other twin showed no symptoms but went down with whatever the ailment was, and it would run its course two to three weeks. At one point, we changed houses, and the twins changed schools. The new school could not take both girls in the same class. The upper class took Julie, and that class was going to the school camp in a week's time.

There were no places left, so Christine could not go. I think the girls were about nine to ten. I can't remember. The camp trip left on a Friday and returned two weeks later. Parents were allowed to visit on the middle Sunday. So Jenn and I decided to go and visit with Christine, of course. At about 10 a.m. on that day, I was walking to our car with Christine. I was holding her hand when she cried out in pain, and I thought she had just stumbled.

As I held her hand, I just simply lifted her up. She said her leg was hurting. By now, Jenn was with us. We put her on the seat in the car while Jenn checked her leg. There was a red weal showing between her knee and hip on the front of her right leg. It was getting deeper in colour (red) and more pronounced. As we were in the car, I drove straight to the doctor's. The surgery was shut, but the doctor came to the car and looked at Christine's leg.

He spoke to Christine and then told us, 'Christine is fine. Where is Julie?' Jenn told him she was at school camp thirty miles away. He told Jenn to come in and phone the camp. When she got a connection, someone at the camp told her Julie was in sickbay. She had been kicked by a pony earlier. Jenn said, 'Was it her right leg above the knee?'

'Yes,' came the reply.

'Please tell Julie, Mum and Dad will be there in one hour.' When we got back to the car and looked at Christine's leg, the imprint of a horseshoe was there in all its glory, nail-holes and everything visible. Julie recovered during the second week. So both girls were fine. Lots of other things have happened with the girls, but none serious enough to worry about.

There were more events that happened before long. The fighting was so bad on the job I was frightened in case I hit someone with a heart complaint and they died.

Paperwork called part 2 orders were put on the noticeboards every week. They informed us of any new laws and any old laws repealed. They also updated news of positions vacant within the force. They were asking for volunteers to start up a dog section, and anyone could apply. I applied and got the job, which meant going on a course with Durham County Force for three months, 9 p.m.–5 p.m., with weekends off.

But it wasn't starting for a month. So instead of posting me on another beat, since a civil defence course for a couple of weeks was available, I went on that. This meant the force had to form a mobile column in case of a nuclear fallout. The column would be self-contained and would include sixty officers in transits and cars, catering vehicle lorries. Sergeants, inspectors, and mechanics would all be together in the event of an atomic bomb attack.

We would go to a designated area in the country and return into the urban areas and police the area from the column. The bosses expected

85 per cent desertion, so it was fingers crossed that no bombs fell in the country.

I returned to work on the east side of High Street and was confronted with a group of people, males and females. They were occupying the seats and grass area outside the Trinity Church. I only had two weeks to get rid of this lot before the dog course started.

I had been forewarned they had arrived about a week ago. They were all about love and peace, and all wore flowery clothing, no socks, just sandals, like flower power people. My boss at the HQ warned me to get rid of them, or I would be disciplined and possibly fined. Some had been arrested for shoplifting during the day, and some for drunkenness during the pub hours. There were between twenty to twenty-five of them.

At about 11 p.m., I was observing them from the other side of the church. There was horseplay, noise, and bad language. I decided it was time to move them. I came around to the High Street and was met with them, taking the mickey out of me. I ignored it and stood in amongst them. Then I told them it was time to move on. This brought out their barrack-room lawyer, a spokesman who told me what I could and could not do according to the law.

Also, he said that they were law-abiding citizens whose taxes paid my wages. I felt so enlightened I asked them to clear the area ASAP. At the side of the church was an alley leading to a public toilet for male and female. They were supposed to be locked by an official from the council before 11.30 p.m. as it was the only convenient time open after the pubs closed. It was usually busy until after midnight.

Nobody came to lock it most nights. Earlier in my posting, I had two keys cut to fit the locks. After watching these people for a few days, it seemed before they moved on, more than half would visit the loos. I followed a couple of stragglers one night, and they went down the back of the High Street to a boarded-up pub. I saw them go in. On my six-to-two shift, I checked the pub out and found all their sleeping bags and personal gear.

There was a strong smell of petrol in the air. A member of the public reported a fire in the pub around ten thirty. I wandered up to the High Street when I got to the church, and sure enough, the mocking and mickey taking continued. After a few more minutes, a fire engine came past. They turned their attention to this and were taking the mickey, telling me I should go with the Trumpton crowd and help them.

I suggested they might want to follow the fire engine because the pub they were sleeping in was on fire. This caused chaos in the group. Some believed me; some didn't. However, most of the group went into the loos, and I just walked up and locked them in. I disappeared to the opposite side of the High Street and went to see how the fire engines were getting on. The leading fireman told me it was arson. That explained the petrol smell.

Some of the hippies/Jesus people were trying to get into the pub and giving the firemen hassle. Soon the traffic lads got involved, and several of the Jesus people were locked up for affray and assault on the firemen. I went into HQ and saw the barrack-room lawyer telling the rest of the bunch their rights. When he saw me, he said, 'Isn't that correct, Officer?'

I replied, 'It must be, if you're saying it, but you could advise them on shoplifting, assault, causing an affray, and drunkenness, all of the above with the ways and means act.'

I went back to the pub. The firemen were packing up but told me they would leave a man at the pub to make sure it didn't start again. I finished my shift without going to the church area and went home. On my next shift, I saw the remains of the pub being knocked down for safety, and when I got to the church, all was quiet. Not a single Jesus follower in sight. The toilets were open at 6 a.m., and the councilman let about twenty of the mob out. They were nowhere on my patch.

My sergeant and inspector visited me and commented how quiet it was. Nothing more to say. Rumours and jokes about the followers were flying about everywhere I went. On another occasion I was on duty at

HQ and was taking my break/cup of tea and sandwiches, the station officer came in and told me there were two senior detectives coming in, and I was to go with them. They had snapped their fingers, and everyone had to jump.

They came in and said they were going to a job and needed a uniformed officer. These two, Detective Inspector Charlie Brown and Chief Superintendent Kent, had long service time in and commanded a great deal of respect throughout the force. To me they looked like Dick Tracy and Sherlock Holmes. We left the station and went to the multistory block of flats. They did not tell me what the job was; they said it might be a sudden death and asked if I was prepared and trained to give CPR, the kiss of life.

As we got near, I could see smoke coming out of the windows on the sixth floor. We went up to the floor by the lift, and when the lift door opened, it immediately filled with thick smoke. I dropped on to my hands and knees and looked under the smoke. There was a clear area of about two feet from the floor up then dense smoke. We made our way along the passage, staying below the smoke. The smell was of horrific burning flesh.

I had smelt this before at fires. We arrived at a door halfway along. I pushed it open further and looked into the room. I could see a woman lying on the floor with her back to me. DC Charlie Brown said, 'Go on. Get in there, and don't forget CPR or the kiss of life.' I crawled to the woman, put my hand on her shoulder which just crumbled, and her head fell off and rolled away. Charlie Brown said, 'There's still a chance. Give her the kiss of life.' And they both just laughed at me.

By now, more windows and doors had been opened, and the smoke was getting thinner. I could see the woman was glowing in her chest and stomach area, and I realised she was cuddling an electric fire. I warned the others and located the plug and pulled it out. The doctor and the coroner's officer arrived, as well as the scenes of crime officers (SOCO). I worked out from a piece of silver paper that the woman was a smoker, because in most cigarette packs, there was silver paper attached to the tissue in the packs. By using this and rolling it out, you could make a taper to light a ciggy. I could also see the electric fire had a join in the coil spring element. The woman had bent down and tried to light the tissue end, but she had held it the wrong way and had touched the electric element with the silver paper.

This gave the lady an electric shock and shorted out the fire. She then fell on to the portable fire, and the movement of the fire reconnected the power. She must have cuddled the fire, and it just burnt out all her insides from the waist up, hence the smell. The detective decided no foul play was suspected; they would turn the case over to the coroner's officer to complete.

The detectives did not say much to me but put in a very good report to the CC as I was just out of probation. They expected me to have been sick or possibly pass out. On a separate occasion, the same two detectives borrowed me from HQ to accompany them on a suicide enquiry. It was also at the multistory flat. We arrived and took the lift to the sixteenth floor. From then on, the builders were working, so it was up the concrete stairs without handrails.

We came out on to the roof. I could see a huge crane coming up the outside of the twenty-one-story flat, and the swinging arm of the crane was about six feet high from the roof and stretched across the building and protruded over the edge of the roof. And on the end was a guy. He had climbed on to the crane and worked his way up to the end. He was known to the CID and to Charlie personally.

They were trying to be nice and talked him into climbing down. I was told to stop anyone else coming on to the roof. There were materials and bricks everywhere. The guy was in a bad, hysterical state and was threatening to jump. At first the detectives were very sympathetic and really tried hard to talk him down. After thirty minutes, they changed attitude and told him, 'We could not waste time, so either come down or we will knock you down.'

They began to throw things at him. Some of which hit him. He decided he would climb down. He came back along the crane and lowered himself on to the roof beside Charlie, who really laid into him and warned him what would happen if he had to come back. He took this guy to the exit and told him to run. Then he turned to me, got hold of my tunic, ripped it open, and pulled some buttons off.

The other one took my helmet and stamped on it and walked to the edge of the roof. He threw it down where traffic cops were watching the door and shouted, 'Prisoner escaped!' Then he joined us and said, 'This nutter attacked you, and we arrested him, but he escaped from us. When we get to HQ, go and tell your sergeant you need some new uniform and a helmet. We will submit the paperwork for you. Get back to your work ASAP.' It upset me so much; I spoke to several sergeants, and their advice was, 'Keep quiet, say nothing. What happened was totally wrong, but if you report this, you will be out of work very soon.' These CID men were a law unto themselves, and I was not experienced enough to take them on. I let it go. About two weeks after that, I was summoned to see the CC. I thought, *Oh no, this time I've had it. He will give me the boot.*

Upon entering his office, he said, 'Come in, have a seat. I have been hearing good things about you from CID. They were impressed by your actions when the lady was burnt and more glowing reports on how you talked a suicide candidate out of going ahead even after you were assaulted. Well done, young man. It gives me great pleasure to tell you I am giving you a commendation for your bravery. Keep up the good work.'

I left his office in a complete spin. I was off duty and talked it over with Jenn. We decided to leave well alone. The suicide man didn't go through with it, so it ended well. It took a long time for me to come to terms with something that went totally against the grain. In fact, I don't think I ever came to terms with it. My attention was drawn to the blue light flashing on the box.

'HQ informed me you have a flasher.' He exposed himself near the shop in the park. I went to the shop, and members of the public pointed a man out to me. It was a nice sunny afternoon, and this chap was wearing a mackintosh buttoned up to his neck. I spoke to him and asked him to come to the box so I could interview him and he could help me with my enquiries. He agreed and stood up. His mac opened as he got up, and I could see he was only wearing leggings that stopped above his knees and held by elastic.

Nothing else. I told him I was arresting him in view of what I had just seen. He was very quiet. We returned to the box. I had to move in front of him because my key to the box was on a short chain. I opened the door and felt an almighty thump on the back of my neck, enough to send me flying into the box and into two cycles, which I got entangled in. By the time I got to my feet, my prisoner was long gone.

Two women were at the door; they said they were the original complainants. I took the emergency phone and handed it to them, telling them to tell the operator what had happened. They also pointed in the direction he had run. I left the women and gave chase after my prisoner. I ran into the back street of Rodsley Avenue and Coatsworth Road. I saw the prisoner walking up the back alley ahead of me. He heard me coming, and he disappeared into an opening on my right.

I ran in, and he was waiting for me, no way out. He started fighting with me. We pushed and rolled about on the ground. I could not detain him long enough to cuff him. I ended up on my knees and made a grab for something to help me to stop him. I could hear voices, and I saw my prisoner fall in a heap behind me. Someone grabbed my collar, lifted me up, and said, 'Leave him to me. Pull yourself together.' It was a motorcycle officer nicknamed Cheyene. He is six feet, seven inches tall and in full motorcycle kit and helmet.

He looked like Darth Vader. The prisoner was taken back to the box. He eventually went to court and was given a small fine of £50. I suffered a broken finger, the last joint on my little finger. He has bitten it and broke it. At 2.30 a.m. on a different occasion, I was sent to the Royal British Legion Club premises. It was situated above a block of four shops. I checked the rear and side doors; both were locked.

So I had gone to the front door. It was also locked. I had not heard the arrival of anyone else, and I saw through the letterbox a guy with a torch coming down the stairs. He was obviously going to leave. I stood up. At this point, an officer crashed through the door, splitting it down the middle. The left half fell into the passage, and the other half swung on its hinges. It was hit so hard it hit the guy coming down the stairs and knocked him out clean. The officer and I lifted the burglar up and took him to a waiting car.

The officer who had arrived was Cheyene. He took the mickey and said that he was sick of rescuing me and that it was time I stood on my own. These two instances took place in my early days before the dog section was set up. He was right; he also rescued me at a dance hall fight, where six were taken into custody. He had no set beat, and I liked the freedom he had. He just went where he thought he could be of help.

He became a good friend off duty as well as on duty. His family lived upstairs to Jenn's parents, and his sister, WPC DC Beatrice Lambert, joined the force and opted for detective work. She was also a good friend of Jenn's. They grew up together.

Ghost on Sunderland Road haunted house

Having used the word *haunted*, it triggered a memory of a house on the Sunderland Road beat. I had heard about this house and the various stories that were told about it. At this time, I did not believe in ghosts or ghouls or banshees or poltergeists or anything of that nature. I was having a break (night shift) at one; I was in the police box. A knock on the door prompted me to get up. I opened the door, and an elderly woman with a heavy street coat over her nightie was there.

I brought her in and sat her in front of the fire and asked her, 'What brings you here at this hour?'

She said, 'It's back, and we can't sleep.' She lived in a downstairs flat with her husband, whom she had left in bed. She explained the ghost was in the kitchen, and it moved the cooker on to the other wall to where it used to be. I looked outside to see if anyone else was there. I thought she was having a laugh and pulling my leg.

However, my break was over, so I said, 'I will walk you home and have a look.' She never stopped talking all the way, about five minutes away. When we arrived at her home, she said she was not frightened of the ghost. Anyway, we went in, and she led me into the kitchen and put a light on. It was small and square. On one wall was a table and two chairs, and on the back wall was the biggest, heaviest cast iron cooker I have ever seen.

The woman said the cooker should be over there and pointed to an empty gap. There were years of grease on the walls around an empty space where the cooker used to be. A lead pipe had been pulled from the wall brackets and had been reshaped to the new position. I turned on a burner and lit the gas. It was all in good working order. I said to the lady, 'I would look around the flat and outside, to see if anything was going on elsewhere.'

She said, 'You will not find anything. It's always just the cooker.' There was only her and her husband living there, and he had gone to bed. I checked all around the outside yard, thinking someone was stirring the old people up. I tried to move the cooker. It was so heavy I reckon; maybe four men might have lifted it. I came in from the yard into the kitchen, and I closed the door.

I still had my hand on the latch when I felt and heard a loud pounding on the door. It startled me, but when I opened the door, no one was there. I rechecked the yard area and checked above the door—nothing to see. I went in and shut the door. The woman said, 'Leave it until tomorrow, and the cooker will be back over there.' I took hold of the latch on the door to open it. The pounding started again. It was so severe that bits of plaster were falling from the sides of the doorposts.

I still had hold of the latch and thought even I couldn't hit the door that hard, and I felt it would fall in, frame and everything. I pulled the door open. The noise stopped, and there was no one there. I looked around the yard area; it was empty. The lady said, 'Come in now. It won't come back until tomorrow.' I came in and shut the door, then bolted it. After talking to the lady and trying to reassure her there was no one there, she just said, 'It's all right now. I will just go to bed.'

I left the house and stood over the street, watching until I saw the light go out. I did not want to leave because I didn't understand what was happening. Eventually, I left. I checked with the other people who had been out on that beat. They had similar experiences and did not have any answers for me. I was on day shift and went back to the flat and saw the lady who reassured the cooker was back in its place.

The next day, as she said it would be, I went in and had a look. Sure enough, the cooker was in its original place, and the lead gas pipes were refixed to the wall. I was posted to another beat and heard later that the husband had died and the lady had a priest exorcise the flat and that no further occurrences had been reported. The experience for me has never been explained—why, how, or what caused the pounding on the door?

Because of that, I keep an open mind. If you have not experienced this type of paranormal behaviour, don't knock it.

I have added another couple of incidents which I attended, like industrial accidents and murders. An employee of a large munitions factory was injured at work. He was employed as a centre lathe turner. This is a huge machine with a working area of ten feet. It is also connected to and cannot operate if the machine in the assembly line in front is not started and working already. Nor can the next machine in line operate if this machine has been switched off.

I only learned this in hindsight. I also learned that once one machine is switched off, the whole lot systematically stops. The buildings housing these machines were vast, and it would take two days to get all the machines working again. I was directed to machine 224 in building 18. Once there, I saw a man sitting in a chair. There was a bucket next to him, and his right arm was missing from the elbow.

The bucket was for catching the blood. The injured man had a couple of mates with him, comforting him and reassuring him while waiting for an ambulance. I asked the mates what had happened. They told me they found him passed out on the floor and got him into the chair. I confirmed which machine he was operating. They said 224. I asked, 'Can you stop it? I want to recover his arm if I can and get it in ice.'

They said, 'Hit the *red* button on the panel.' Which I did, and the machine came to a stop. I searched around the area but could not see the victim's arm anywhere. The paramedics turned up after fifteen minutes. As did men in office suits who were the blue-collar workers. One said, 'Who has stopped the machine?'

I said, 'I did, and who are you?' They told me they were the bosses of this section and that all the sections were stopped and at a standstill.

Other machine operators were coming to check on the injured man. One boss asked me why I stopped the machine. I replied, 'I had to so I could search for the injured man's arm without any danger from the machine.'

He said, 'Come with me.' And we went to the injured man. The boss lifted his raggy torn sleeve, and I could see a cut in the muscle of the injured man's arm, which was bleeding.

The boss said, 'This man was injured in France during the war, and that is where his arm is. Now the whole plant is at a standstill for two days. Thank you very much, Officer.' The medics dressed the injured man's arm but decided he did not need further treatment. I left quietly. As I was approaching the outside gate, I saw a huge gang of men all waving and shouting at me, cheering.

I waited till they were with me. They were all machine operators and were going home for at least two days' paid leave because of the shutdown. I left them and returned to work.

That incident reminded me of another confrontation with workers. I was sent to Swan Hunter's shipyard at 9 a.m. one Monday morning. Hunter's is about fifteen to twenty minutes away from HQ in Gateshead, and I was on my own.

I drove as near as I could but had to abandon my car as the traffic was at a standstill. There were crowds everywhere in the area. I walked with some of the men and asked what was going on. This worker told me that five shipyards had closed their gates on Friday gone, and all these workers had to report to Swan's yard to see which yards were working and which were not working.

Each of the yards employed 10,000 workers and worked shift work 24/7. So night workers for Friday, Saturday, and Sunday plus early/late shift workers for three days had all come to Swan's to see if they were still employed. There were angry scuffles which turned into fighting in the crowd. Because Swans could not cope with the numbers, they had to lock the workers out. I was allowed to pass through the gate as the crowd were not anti-police. I spoke to the managers and learned that they had decided to close five yards forever.

All employees from those yards were now redundant. The bosses had decided that the managers and owners would go to their yards and open the offices to the workers' representatives, foremen, and union reps to explain what would happen to the men in the future. This was relayed to the crowds who made their way to their own yards for the meetings. More and more traffic officers arrived, but the crowd slowly dispersed, except for 50–60 men who worked at Swan's. They were allowed in.

I made my way to another yard, but it was not required. It was orderly. It was all a bit unnerving to be faced with up to 45,000-50,000 workers. It was like the turnout of a football match. Five shipyards did close with the loss of thousands of jobs. The whole area of the northeast was dying. Coal mines were closing; heavy industry was closing. Steelworks, engineering—they were all shutting down.

People were desperate for work. Some employers restricted to only one family member to work for them. All jobs like window cleaners, taxi drivers, and bus drivers were being taken by skilled workers to feed their families. Crime rates went higher and higher. It was the policy that all industrial accidents had to be attended to by the police to make sure that there was no foul play involved.

I recall three incidents I was sent to. Two resulted in death—one of which was a murder—and for the third, there were no injuries, just mayhem. I will start with a call to a steelyard, where men working in the yard stacking steel slabs utilised a crane to unload the lorries and lifted steel slabs by means of chains to the top outer corners. The slabs of steel were four inches thick and were eight feet high and twelve feet long; each one weighed ten tons.

They were being stacked by lowering them until the bottom long edge was touching the ground in front of the last one laid. The crane would still have control of the plate until a couple of men on the ground, one at each end of the plate, would push it backwards as the crane eased the weight off. It would be tilted over, ready to lean on the last plate laid. The men would then release the chains for the crane to get the next plate, and this plate would fall back a couple of inches to rest perfectly flat on the last one laid.

Only this time, it had gone wrong. There was a problem with the chains being released, and a man had gone on to the stack of slabs to try to release the chains for the crane to be able to move. One of the chains snapped. The guy on top of the plates was knocked into the gap, and the plate fell into place against the last one. The men worked desperately to prise the plates apart, but without success.

The longer it took, the lesser chance the guy trapped would be alive. One worker brought a JCB with a bucket on the front to try and hook the bucket on to the top of the plate, pull it forward, and let it fall flat on the ground. He managed at the second attempt. By now, all the yard workers were coming to help. The ambulance was on stand by and the fire brigade en route.

As the gap opened between the plates, I could see a bundle of clothing looking like it had been screwed up in a heap, and the whole plate was awash with blood from corner to corner, top to bottom. I instantly vomited, as did several others. We were all taken care of by the paramedics. The guy on the plate lost his life being crushed to death. This was recorded as death by misadventure.

I was sent home and given a day off the next day. On the next incident, no one was hurt. But it could have been a massacre. It was eight thirty, and I was on a school crossing duty until ten past nine, just in case any late stragglers came. The crossing was in two parts with a central reservation in between dual carriageways. A lorry turned into Sunderland Road, and I heard chains snapping.

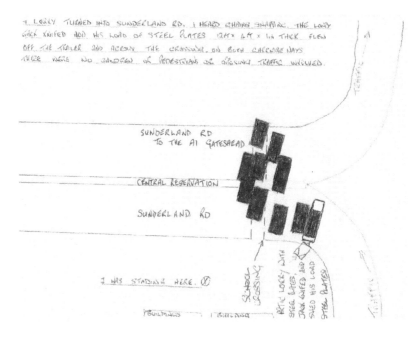

The lorry jack knifed, and his load began to fly off the trailer like a pack of cards. They flew across the school crossing and both carriageways. The sheets were thin but were twelve feet by six feet and one inch thick. Ten sheets flew off when the securing chains snapped. Luckily, no schoolchildren or pedestrians were about and no opposing traffic while the sheets were flying. No one was hurt.

The driver was prosecuted for an unsecured load. Traffic officers were quickly on site and took control. The road was cleared in a couple of hours. Thank God no children were hurt. I was still shaking and trembling when I went home at four thirty after seeing the children over the dual carriageway, which had been cleared and the lorry removed.

The third incident was a murder involving two bakers working at a large dough-making machine in a huge bakery.

One forced the other into the machine and set it going. The man inside was killed. The other one was arrested for murder. The details were too gory for me to write out. I was off work for two days being ill after that one.

On two other occasions, I was called to a coal depot on the edge of an industrial estate in Gateshead. There were a few residential houses nearby. The depot was only partially used, and the fences were falling down or missing. This area was frequented by prostitutes because of easy access to the coal yard and open sheltered areas, out of the eyes of the residents.

On the first occasion, it was a murder. The victim was found by depot employees. They showed me where the body was. It was a young female who had been brutalised. She had obviously put up a struggle and was only half dressed; she had been dragged where she lay. She was unrecognisable because her face had been smashed with a fifty-six-pound weight, and a huge lump of coal had been pounded into her skull so that no part of her face could be seen, just this lump of coal pounded into her skull. I checked her wrist but could not find a pulse. She was dead, but only a doctor could certify death.

I called out the teams, and the scene was preserved as best I could. CID officers turned up as well as scenes of crime officers. The coroner's officer and the doctor turned up. CID took over the enquiries. The doctor certified the death. The coroner's officer organised the removal of the body to the morgue beside the swing bridge. As far as I am aware, no assailant had been found.

The second time I was called to this location was nearly a year later. This also was a female in her thirties. She too had been sexually assaulted and brutalised and was dead. I had moved on and was now a dog handler. The officers dealing with the case thought the dog might pick up a track to follow. I examined the body and the immediate surroundings. This lady had been sexually assaulted and brutalised.

The perpetrator had placed some large empty bottles neck first into the vagina and then hammered them into her body with a twenty-eight-pound hammer. There was broken glass protruding from her stomach and side and back and right up under her rib cage. I searched the yard with the help of the dog, and he led me to where the bottles and the hammer used had been kept. These articles were bagged and tagged and handed to SOCO, who tested them for fingerprints.

The post-mortem report said all major organs had been damaged by glass. The good news was, a match had been found with the prints left on the hammer. A man was arrested and charged with murder. Just another day at the office.

The boss's new car

I was about to go off duty at Gateshead HQ at 2 p.m. when I was asked to do the duty sergeant a favour and get a couple of hours overtime. I agreed, and transport was arranged to take me to Whickham. It was about eight to ten miles out of town. I was to pick up a brand-new car which had radio equipment fitted to it. It was an AUSTIN 1800 and was designated for use by duty inspectors.

The engineer showed me where the main unit was fitted in the boot; he showed me how to remove this unit and explained it must not be left in the car anywhere outside the radio range. He demonstrated how the handset worked and that it was all tuned in to receive message from Gateshead HQ. I left the radio workshop and drove towards Gateshead. The radio was still on. It was a lovely new car in pristine condition, and I loved the size of it and the smell of new leather.

My daydreaming was short-lived. When I was entering the Gateshead boundary, the radio came to life. The operator was calling for any vehicle in the Lobley Hill area. There was no response, and I was only a couple of miles away and approaching the area. After two more calls, no other cars answered, so I responded, saying, 'HQ, I am PC160 en route to Gateshead in a new and as yet unmarked car which has no call sign. I am in uniform. Can I help?'

The reply came, saying, 'Stand by, PC160. PC160, from HQ, you are authorised to drive to Coach Road just off Lobley Hill. WHEN YOU ENTER THE COACH ROAD, THE FIRST 200 YARDS HAS LARGE TREES ON EITHER SIDE. PICK TWO TREES OPPOSITE EACH OTHER AND PARK YOUR CAR ACROSS THE ROAD BETWEEN THE TREES TO MAKE A BARRIER, THEN GET OUT AND LEAVE THE CAR QUICKLY.'

I replied, 'You realise this is the inspector's new car!'

'HQ TO PC160, THIS IS THE DUTY INSPECTOR, AND THIS IS AN INSTRUCTION, NOT A REQUEST. THERE IS A STOLEN CAR HEADING YOUR WAY. IT IS CLOSE. GET OUT OF THE DAMN CAR, OVER.'

'PC160 ten 4. I left the car and took cover behind a tree away from the car. At this time, I could hear two tones coming towards me.' About 100 yards ahead of me, the road dipped downhill. By now, the stolen car was very near. The pursuit cars had been alerted to my barrier.

The cars came flying up out of the dip. The stolen car was so close he was looking at a choice of piling into my car or the trees either side. He chose to ram my car out of the way, but the impact caused his car to climb over mine. As it was now starting to roll, the stolen car went skyward and came down front grill into the road and landed on its roof, as did my car. The pursuit cars had time to brake and stop before reaching the wreckage. They were CID officers in unmarked cars. The debris stopped flying, and the noise stopped.

The driver was arrested and taken to the hospital. The other CID driver organised traffic cars to come and deal with the wreckage. My car and the stolen car had to be picked up and taken to HQ. I removed the magic radio equipment from the wreck. The car was a write-off. CID gave me a lift to HQ. I handed in the radio box and the keys and told the officer the car would be in the yard within the hour. Then I left for home. Four hours overtime in the bag.

On another incident on the Sunderland Road beat, I was on night duty and was in the police box taking refreshments. There was a knock on the door, which I opened carefully, as it was 1.30 a.m. I was confronted by two males; the younger one had serious facial injuries.

The older one looked like a military type, approximately forty-five years old. My concern was with the younger man in his early twenties. His cheekbones were broken, and his right eye socket bones were broken. They were jabbering at each other, so I got a grip of the situation by picking up the emergency phone and handing it to the older one. He struck me as odd because his right hand was in his blazer pocket, and he had to turn to reach the phone with his left hand. I instructed him to tell the operator I required an ambulance ASAP, and I also required assistance at Sunderland Road box.

I used the first-aid kit and cleaned up the lad's face; I made some padding and asked the lad to hold it in place on his wounds. The older man was becoming more agitated and was crowding me. I stepped back and told the older one to sit down away from us. It was obvious they had been fighting each other from what they were arguing about. The older one stood up, and I pushed him away from me. I said, 'Let me look at your hand. You must be injured.' He removed his hand from his pocket and took a swing at me.

I sidestepped the blow as his hand went past my face. He hit the side of the box, and his arm went straight through the wooden panels right up to his elbow. I just leant on him and held him there because I could hear a traffic car nearby. I put handcuffs on his left hand and pulled him back into the box; I fastened the other part of the cuffs on to a steel bar over the rear window and quickly took hold of his right arm. His right hand was missing, and the stump was fitted with a steel cuff to halfway up his forearm.

It was an old injury, and the steel was designed to accept other gadgets like cutlery and tools like a screwdriver. I turned my attention to the young lad and asked, 'Is this how you got your injuries?'

He nodded. 'Yes.' The ambulance and the traffic PC arrived. The medics took the lad to the hospital. The prisoner was taken to HQ and charged with GBH (grievous bodily harm) and assault on me.

It took a long time for the lad to heal. The older man was his uncle, and after being examined by doctors who took his mental state into consideration, the Crown Prosecution Service decided to drop the charge of assault on me and reduce the GBH charge to common assault provided he would receive treatment for his mental well-being.

On another night on Sunderland Road—it was a bitter cold winter night—I had arranged with the night shift baker working in one of the local shops to call in about 4 a.m. so I could get warmed up. This was one of the four shops on the main road quite close to the police box. This practice had been going on for a long time; the baker had been there for years. He knew most of the men and all the sergeants and inspectors by name. He also knew if I was caught skiving, it would mean disciplinary action or a fine or both.

I turned up at 4 a.m., and the baker had a hot cup of tea and some freshly baked scones with butter waiting for me. Once inside, he asked, 'Have you had your visit from the inspector and sergeant?' I just shook my head no. He then locked the main door so no one could just walk in on us. We enjoyed the tea and food, and we had stopped talking until he asked, 'What time do you ring in?'

'Three minutes to the hour,' I said.

'You better get your skates on. It's gone 5 a.m.'

There was a knock on the door, and a voice asked, 'Mr Baker, have you seen my beat man?'

The baker let me out into the rear yard as he replied, 'Coming, Inspector.' And he opened the front door to my boss.

I decided not to go out into the rear lane, and instead, I jumped over the wall into the next yard and kept going over the next wall and once again over the last wall into the last yard. What a stroke of luck! I landed on top of a burglar who was making off down the yard with his loot. He had burgled the pawnshop. I grabbed him and opened the door and took him on to the main road.

I could see the inspector waiting outside the box. It was less than 100 yards away, but he sent his driver to give me a hand. We took the prisoner to the box and called out the keyholder to the shop to make it secure. The boss checked my book and signed it. He said, 'We will take your prisoner to HQ. You can come in your own car and go home from there once you have him under lock and key and notified CID he is here. Good work, young man. Keep it up.' He left, and I went to see the baker, and we enjoyed a good laugh. I completed all my work at HQ and went home to bed.

While working the town beat in Gateshead on night shift, it covered the riverside area to Swan Hunter's yard, way past Spillers Flour Mill. It was a well-known area and has now been developed into a great sports arena and a vast open area for all kinds of sports.

I was sent to the area to check on a report of gunfire heard there. I searched the area and located two officers who were drunk. They had been given the job of taking the unused ammunition to the army range and firing it off before the new consignment arrived at the armoury. These two idiots were given the job before noon and had chosen to go drinking instead.

It was now 11 p.m. They had forgotten about the guns and ammo until the pub closed and, in their drunken wisdom, decided to get rid of the ammo by firing it on to the river. From where we were, there was a left-hand bend in the river as you go towards the sea; it was about 200 yards away. Either side of the river was flanked by working shipyards with men working the night shift. The two drunken idiots soon got bored and started firing into the river and then at the navigation lights in various places at the bend of the river.

The bullets were overshooting into the steel hulls on the Newcastle side of the river, where men were working. I immediately disarmed the pair of them and made the weapons safe and secured in my car boot. I called the traffic car and had these men escorted to HQ under arrest. I had the weapons placed in the armoury, and I had the car brought into HQ. The two men were charged and held overnight in the cells until the next day. CID officers took over the case because I was not experienced enough to know it would never get to court.

An internal enquiry decided *one* of the men would be reduced in rank from sergeant to constable, and the other PC resigned and immigrated to Australia, but not before they went to court on lesser charges. They still had to pay substantial fines. Word went around the force very quickly that I had arrested two colleagues. This action had never been known for years. All police personnel were very wary when working with me; they all knew for sure I would not hesitate to arrest any wrongdoer, police or otherwise.

I was on duty on the Sunderland Road beat and was in a police box taking my refreshments at 1.30 a.m. All the local people know that an officer would be at the box at that time, so they knew for sure they would get help without having to wait for someone to be sent. There was a knock on the door, and I thought, *There goes my break time.* I opened the door to a woman in her forties; she was hysterical and shouting at me that her sister was being killed by her husband. I managed to calm her long enough to get an address, then I called HQ for assistance. I walked with the woman who was still very agitated and worried about her sister. We soon arrived at the house.

I was shown into a front bedroom. There was a big man naked, lying face down on the bed. I could not see anyone else and asked, 'Where is your sister?' She was getting more hysterical again and telling me she was under her husband, and she bent down on one knee and pointed under the bed. I could see the bedframe was broken right up the middle, and the weight of these two had created a large hold. Their bodies had forced the mattress through the hole, and it was touching the floor. Another officer arrived, and we tried to lift the man up. He was too big and too heavy; he was also *dead*.

We decided to dismantle the frame, and we both heaved on the side and upended the whole thing on to the floor.

We were able to pull the thin mattress through the hole, and this exposed the naked sister who was also in a hysterical state, alive but still attached, impaled by her husband. She could not get free and get up yet. The PC and I moved all the debris—broken bedframe and mattress—to give us a bit of space. I ended up sitting on the floor over the husband's head. He was now lying on his back, with my feet on his shoulders. I reached down and took hold of the sister's hand. She was small and frail. I was about to pull her towards me and try to free her from her husband. She stopped the hysterics for a second, looked at me, and said gently.

My mind flashed to thoughts of home and Jenn, and I started to giggle. I thought, *She is never in a hundred years going to believe this.* And at the same time, I pulled the lady towards me because the other PC was at the other end, and I had visions of him pushing her backside to help free her. I started to laugh. I freed the lady from her dead husband. She got up and left the room. I broke into fits of laughter with the other PC. We still had the dead man to deal with.

Again, we called the doctor to certify the death and the coroner's officer who made arrangements to have the body taken to a chapel of rest as there were no suspicious circumstances.

The doctor concluded the couple were having intercourse, and the husband had a heart attack. The result was, they were trapped in the base of the bed. The ladies were seen by the doctor and deemed to be okay. As the doctor left, he said to me, 'You must learn to control your laughter. It is not dignified.' And he left. I could hear him laughing as he went along the passage.

The ladies came back into the sitting room; they were carrying tea and biscuits. They were now quite composed, but stark naked. They explained that they were strippers and were working the northern clubs. They explained being naked at home made it easier for them when they were at work.

The wife of the dead man had completely composed herself and thanked us for freeing her from her husband. They showed no remorse at all for the dead husband. I was in stitches with laughter and apologised for laughing. The PC and I left the house, and I went to the police box to finish my tea break and sandwiches.

This incident always brings a smile when I think about it. That's what I like about my job. You never know what's going to happen next. Every incident I attend, I ask myself a few questions.

1. Am I walking into danger? Are my men at risk?
2. Is my job at risk if I get it wrong?
3. Can I get glory and praise out of this and be a hero?
4. Is there a serious possibility of discipline charges if I get it wrong?

I can only revert to training and experiences to help me get it right, and I have to remember the reason I am here.

THE CUSTOMERS ARE THE WRONGDOERS AND ARE NEVER RIGHT.

IT WORKS FOR ME.

CHAPTER TWO

The time came for me to go to Durham County and begin a training course on dog handling. We were still living opposite Jenn's mum, so she had plenty of help with the young family, and I could get home at nights. The period covered four years. At this time, I bought my first car—a Ford Popular. I reported to the mounted and dog section and went through the course's welcome speeches by the ranking officers in charge.

In the afternoon, I was taken to the kennels and given a dog called King.

He was to work with me; he became mine from that point. He was a German shepherd dog or Alsation. I was issued with leads, choke chains, etc. I met the resident kennel man, a civilian who worked there for many years. He was very good and helped me a great deal during my course.

The two main officers responsible for all aspects of training were Sergeant Regan and PC Gus. They were responsible for the daily programme of training. I found the training relatively easy as I had owned my own Alsation for about a year. I was used to walking, feeding, and housing the dog. The course progressed, and there were lots of incidents, but only three come to mind.

The sergeant and Gus ran a private dog training class for the locals. I found corruption even at this place. They were asking people to donate any GSD that they could not cope with, and they would give them a test to see if they would make good police dogs. Many dogs were handed in but failed tests and were sold to security firms and basically anyone who wanted one. This really went against my ideas of policemen. Guess who made the profit.

The course was nearing the end, and tests were given to find the top dog and handler. King and I were second to a PC from Middlesbrough. Before we went home and just before the tests, the press were doing an article on the establishment. I was asked to run for a dog so they could photograph it, making a capture. The bosses chose a Doberman from the kennel.

My Dog "King" (front row left)

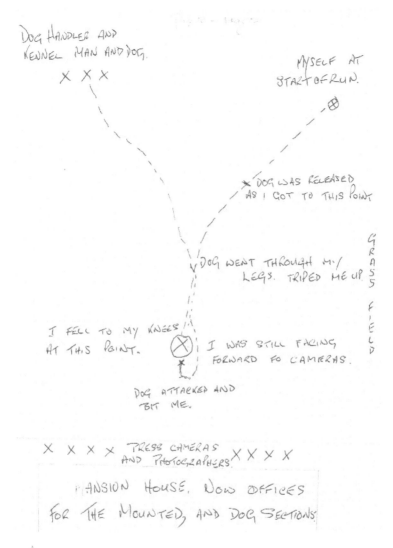

I ran, and when the dog caught up to me, it did not bite the padded sleeve but ran through my legs, and I ended up on my knees and sitting on my ankles. The dog circled me and then attacked me from the front; it was biting and got hold of my penis and testicles. I was fighting and hurting this dog to make it release. The handler was still at the other end of the field. I took hold of the dog's tail and lifted its back legs off the ground. This exposed its nuts.

I grabbed them and applied extreme pressure, which made the dog let go of me. The handler and kennel man arrived and calmed the dog down and led him away. I forgot all about what was going on and dropped my trousers to my ankles so I could inspect the crown jewels carefully. There was a lot of pain and some blood. I could see flashing lights, looked up, and saw all the cameras flashing. I turned my back on them and pulled my pants up.

I left the field and got some first aid. I went home shortly afterwards. The following week, the course ended on Friday. We were allowed to walk the dogs before lunch. In the middle of this walk, three of us released our dogs so they could play and relieve themselves. At one point, all three dogs were out of sight. We called them in and returned to the hall. Regan was waiting for us and instructed me to fasten my dog up at the door and go for my lunch.

He said the vet was checking all the dogs before release. I returned after lunch, and Regan gave me a sack and said, 'Your dog is in the vet's office. It's dead. Put it in the sack and give it to the kennel man.' When I asked what was going on, he was very blunt and said, 'You let your dog off the lead earlier, and the farmer saw it chasing sheep.'

I protested and said, 'There were three dogs together, and they did not have time to chase sheep.'

He cut me short. 'It's done. Now take it away.' He was so smug.

I asked, 'Has anyone phoned Gateshead? I am supposed to be taking a working dog back with me.' Regan's face was a picture when he realised that I was not from his force and that they had killed the chief constable's dog. At 3 p.m., my chief constable turned up in his official car. Regan had assembled his dogs for the chief to look at.

I spoke with the kennel man. He told me Regan had panicked and brought the dogs. 'But if I were you, I would take Elfie. She's just in from Germany and a lovely dog. She's in the kennel.'

My chief constable said, 'Take your pick, Brian.'

I said, 'None of these. I will take Elfie from the kennels.' She was brought out and given to me. I had to return to training on Monday to detrain and retrain Elfie in English. She was very good; I got on very quickly.

The kennel man told me Regan and the bosses were fuming because they had paid so much for this dog. The training was over, and I returned home. Things had been happening at home and at the station. A police house (third home) became available at Southend Road—a three-bedroom house with a terrace at the end of a block of four. I took Jenn to see it, and she loved it. We took it and moved in. It was a much nicer part of town.

A dog van had been added to the fleet and given to me. The boss, inspector of traffic, gave me the keys and said he was now in charge of the dog section, and I would have to answer to him for everything. He became a damn nuisance. So I requested to see the deputy chief. I told him my grievances. He said, 'Brian, you have a free hand. You can use the van twenty-four hours a day as long as there is a dog in it. I will talk to the inspector and put him right. Good luck with the dog. Make it work.'

I had made another enemy in Inspector Paddy 'Fag Ash' McDonald. He tried to get me to report to the garage every time I went out. But that soon faded out. Jenn and I loved that house. It was too far out of town for all the visitors, so I could spend lots of time with Jenn. She met the other wives and made friends.

The beat man's house was back to back with us. He showed interest in the dog, so he would pop in regularly. When he saw me, he would come in. He was the same age as me. His name was also Brian, and he had three youngsters the same as me. I worked with the dog and gained a lot of success in arrests. I was becoming well-known about town.

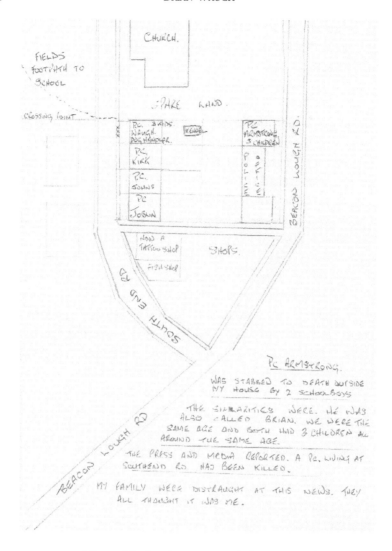

CHURCH.

FIELDS
FOOTPATH TO
SCHOOL

crossing point

SPARE LAND.

PC. BRIDS
WAUGH.
DOG HANDLER.

KENNEL

PC
ARMSTRONG
3 CHILDREN

PC.
KIRK

POLICE

PC.
JOHNS

PC
JOBLIN

NOW A
TATTOO SHOP

SHOPS.

FISH SHOP

BEACON LOUGH RD.

SOUTH END RD

BEACON LOUGH RD

PC ARMSTRONG.

WAS STABBED TO DEATH OUTSIDE
MY HOUSE BY 2 SCHOOLBOYS

THE SIMILARITIES WERE. HE WAS
ALSO CALLED BRIAN. WE WERE THE
SAME AGE AND BOTH HAD 3 CHILDREN ALL
AROUND THE SAME AGE.

THE PRESS AND MEDIA REPORTED. A PC. LIVING AT
SOUTHEND RD HAD BEEN KILLED.

MY FAMILY WERE DISTRAUGHT AT THIS NEWS. THEY
ALL THOUGHT IT WAS ME.

I even suggested I could give lectures and demonstrations at schools. So if the youngsters saw us, they would not to approach the dog if she was out of the van as she was working. It was a huge success. Great PA for the force. I was called into HQ and was told the force was building a substation at the edge of town at Harlow Green. It was expected to be finished in months.

It was four houses and four garages with proper brick kennels attached to the garages. Two houses were earmarked for dog handlers, one for a beat man, and one for a sergeant, with a large car park for police only.

I had requested for us to have a second handler as my workload was really piling up. The watch committee for the force agreed, and the position was advertised.

I had a new car—Morris 1000. (My cousin got it for me; he worked as an agent.) Time had moved on, and one day, I spent all day looking for a couple of grammar school lads about fourteen years old. They were bunking off school and stealing from cars. At 3 p.m., I returned home, put the dog in the kennel, and saw Brian. He was making his way to the school crossing outside my door.

He came in and had coffee, and we could see when the kids came out of school and came to the crossing. When he saw the first few kids, he put his cup away and went to the crossing. After a few minutes, I looked out and could not see him. So I went out to get the kids over the busy road. When I got to the footpath, I saw Brian face down on the path. I shouted for Jenn, and she came out. We turned him over and lifted his head. Jenn cradled him while I got help. He was unconscious.

By the time the ambulance arrived, he had died in Jenn's arms. He was taken to hospital, dead on arrival (DOA). I spoke to some of the mums waiting for their kids and was told Brian had spoken to two grammar school boys and was walking them away. Suddenly, a scuffle started. Brian fell down, and the boys ran off. The boys were wearing scarlet blazers, and their school was at the other end of town.

Word had come back from hospital that Brian had been stabbed with such a force that the blade had severed his aorta. He would have been dead almost instantly. The area now was flooded by PCs and cars, and even off-duty guys were turning up to assist. The grammar school boys were rounded up and detained. They were charged with various charges, and one of the boys with murder.

They were both sent to a secured youth facility and held until they were old enough to go to prison. Rumours were rife. The media did not get the full details but published that 'a PC called Brian with three kids had been stabbed at Southend Road'. I went to my mum's and

Jenn's mum's to reassure them that I was okay and that it was the beat officer who had been killed on my doorstep.

I returned home, and half the force was in my house. The knife used had not been found, so everyone searched the area. I went to the hospital and was given Brian's clothing and uniform. When I checked the pockets of his mac, I found the knife and preserved it for scenes of crime officers (SOCO). It was a very small Smokers knife, the blade only 2.5 inches and only sharp on one side.

This was proven to be the murder weapon. Unbelievable force must have been used to penetrate a raincoat on top of a jacket and to then go through the flap of his tunic pocket through his shirt, vest, and chest and get between his ribs to reach the main artery to his heart and sever the aorta. I can't get my head around this, not then, not now. All kinds of functions were organised to raise money for his widow and children.

The watch committee promised in the media she would be allowed to stay in the home. It turned out to be lies; she and the kids were turfed off within three weeks. Time passed, and we all moved on after the full military funeral. I got rid of the Morris and got a Ford Consul. My working life was about to change, but I did not know it yet until my boss told me a PC had been given the vacant dog handler's job and would be working under me.

It was a guy called Bob. I had worked on the High Street with him, and we had clashed many times. He was senior to me in age and service and had been moved out of every department he served in. This was the only place he had not worked. It was sort of his last chance. He never fit in anywhere and always caused upset and turmoil. I describe him as six foot one and twenty stones.

He worked in the shipyard as a blacksmith's striker in the days before rivet guns. So he could be a handful, not to be underestimated. I continued working as normal. We got word the new substation was ready. We could move into the new-style house (fourth house move). It was known as the butterfly house, different to all the others; the living room was upstairs.

It had gas-powered ducted central heating. One bedroom on one level, with one bathroom, and two bedrooms down a level. There was a kitchen/utility room and toilet on the ground floor. The kids all went to Harlow Green infants school 400 yards down the hill. The no. 4 garage was to be used for the dog van. There was a hatch leading from the first kennel into the garage, so the dog that was on call could come through and get into a cage in the back of the van.

It saved time, and it was just a matter of closing the van door and driving off. Eventually, the beat man and the sergeant moved in. We all got on okay. Jenn teamed up with the beat man's wife, Betty. They became lifelong friends. Bob moved in, and it was awkward. He complained that he should have the sergeant's home which was nearer to the kennels.

He moaned, and his wife and daughter caused friction. His wife was a huge woman, thirty stones. His daughter was eleven years old but was going to the same way as his wife; she was a lovely girl. Notice came through that Bob's course was about to start next week. I called him into my office and told him the news and wished him well. He went on his course, and I got phone calls from the school to tell me he was making himself unpopular in training.

Could I help him get back on track? I did speak to Bob, but it made things worse. I left off, telling Bob about his course. It did not take long before Kevin, the kennel man, was ringing up and asking me why I sent this Bob on a course. He was too old and set in his ways to be around younger men and animals. He had no idea of interacting with others and was disruptive and critical of others.

He had more service time; he tried to tell everyone else they were wrong in their methods. I told Kevin (kennel man) that Bob was not my choice. He had been kicked out of every department he ever worked in, and I was stuck with him. I also warned him about Bob's bullying attitude and temper. I said Regan could stitch him up and have his dog killed the same as he did to me and him thrown off the course.

That solution would solve my problem with him. Bob and I had a word about his training and attitude. He pleaded ignorance of all that was going on around him. Bob also told me he had visited the Crook social club dance on a Wednesday. I took the mickey and told him some of the local girls were only there to secure some dumb copper and secure their futures.

All the girls had a timetable of when a new intake of handlers came in for three months, and all turned up on Wednesday's dances to survey the field. I told him, 'Joking aside, you are on a course and are an ambassador representing Gateshead force. Don't get involved and bring us all into disrepute.' I might as well have been talking to his dog. I visited the school over the next couple of weeks and had meetings with staff because I was in charge of the section at Gateshead.

I relayed all the concerns relative to Bob and his dog to my bosses. No one listened, and they did not care. So everything carried on as before. Notice of the police dog trials were posted, and the dates were for the week after Bob's course ended. My bosses wanted to know if we were good enough to enter. I assured them Bob was telling me he was doing well on his course, and it would be good experience for him.

So I entered him for the trials. When paperwork and acceptance of his entry came. There was no going back. He could not get out of it. I spoke to Bob and said he was going off to the national trials the week after his course. They were to be held in Anwick, north of Newcastle. I expected an argument and protest, but surprise, surprise, he was really pleased and enthusiastic.

He had asked about accommodation and if wives would go for the week if it was in a hotel. Then he told me he had found a girlfriend at Crook, and it would be nice if he could have a week with her as his wife. As you may imagine, a row started and ended with him telling me he would handle all correspondence from now on to do with the dog trials. I handed him the file and said, 'Fill your boots and have a great time.'

He only had a few weeks of his course to finish, and he had told everyone at the school he was entered in the upcoming trials. The phone was jumping off the cradle with dog school staff trying to get him off the trials. I just passed the buck and said it had been authorised by my chief constable. 'Remember the chief who came to the school when you shot his dog?'

No more calls came after that. I found out Bob's girlfriend was a fifty-eight-year-old working hooker, with seven kids. She was near enough double his wife, weighing twenty-five stones, and was coupled with an alcoholic on–off boyfriend, the father of some of her kids. Just how crazy is this situation! He was in love. The staff at the school pleaded with me to cancel his entry to the trials, saying that neither Bob or his dog were anywhere near trial standard of training required.

I said it was all booked and out of my hands. Bob finished the course and came home with his dog. It was not placed in the first six out of nine on the course. I worked his shifts out and kept him on duty when I was off, so I did not work with him or his dog, except on training days. The dog trials came quickly, and off went Bob and his dog. His dog was reportedly vicious and disruptive to other dogs and would fight with them on or off a lead.

Three days into the trials, he was sent home because the dog could not complete the exercises and tests without disrupting other dogs/handlers. The chief constable sent for him, and I thought he would be taken off the section because of the trials and reports I had put in requesting his transfer. Nothing like that happened, and he turned out for work the next day, which was a training day, so I could see for myself the standard he had reached.

The dog was vicious, so I kept mine separate from his as much as possible. Work was coming fast as the force got to utilise the dogs for searching buildings, factories, etc. and for the crowd control on the High Street and football matches. I felt that I had made the right move in accepting the handler's job. Jenn made new friends. The children had all settled in at school.

I had organised a contract with a friend who ran a butcher's shop to supply good steak for the dogs. I purchased two half-size milk churns, and every day I would drop off an empty churn and pick up a full one about 4 p.m. Sometimes Tom (the butcher) would wrap up a few sausages or chops and put them in the churn for me. It was a big help at times, but I had to stop the extras when Bob picked up the dogs' feed.

Money was still poor in the force, and when they stopped paying cash weekly and paid cheques direct into the bank monthly, it made it more difficult to manage. I was on £55 per month, and when we got paid, I owed my mother £20 and Jenn's mum £20. That left me £15 to keep three kids on for a month. So it was not easy to manage. Jenn took on a part-time job when the kids were settled in school. That was a big help.

The cost of living was much different to the present. So £55 was considered good, on a level with doctors and teachers. I worked my days off with a friendly coalman delivering coal all day. It helped quite a bit. Durham County Force had sixty dogs, and I was better off financially by £12 a week in comparison with officers with the same service time as I had.

Time went by, and several incidents made working alongside Bob near impossible. I made out duty rosters which we would work from, and copies were held at HQ so they could contact us quickly. Bob also kept up his liaison with his girlfriend at Crook. If the van was available, he would use it. If not, he would use his own car. On the week he was on call or working a late shift, he would tell his wife he was working nights, take the van and dog to a mate's house, and go to Crook in his mate's car to meet his girlfriend and go to the dance.

It was disrupting the whole system and bringing us a bad name as a dog section. His wife would ask my wife why Bob was always working nights while I did not. Jenn said she better ask him as she had not been promoted or had anything to do with the dog section or police other than be married to me. The rift and atmosphere grew deeper. Envy and resentment all set in.

Trying to run the section and enjoying it became near impossible. The manner in which he talked to and treat the public was a disgrace. Complaints were coming in almost daily to the bosses, and nothing was being done. Opposite were we lived was spare land earmarked for the town to be extended with new homes, but the phase of building had not quite reached us, so I used to let my dog off the lead on this land late at night, give her a chance to clear her system out. Bob knew this and adopted the same for his dog. The new houses being built opposite were very upmarket, and the owners were very well-off. I was called out because of a burglary at one of the houses. The owners had returned home and disturbed the burglar who had ran away over the building site. Bob heard the phone, saw me head over to the new houses, and decided to bring his dog to see if we could pick up a track. I left it to Bob and went to see the householder. I checked the house but left my dog in the van.

I also removed my boots before entering this beautiful home. I was upstairs checking the owner's bedroom with him when the door burst open and Bob's dog ran in, barked ferociously at the owner, and jumped up on to the bed. I managed to quieten it down. It was jumping on and off the bed, and at one stage, it stood in the middle of the bed and shook itself vigorously to remove all the mud and water.

It had rolled in on the building site, and water splashed and sprayed all over the bedroom, up the walls on the ceiling, carpets, and furniture. Bob came in, and I instructed him to remove his dog immediately. He smelt of booze, gave me an argument about ordering him about, then he walked out and called the dog to him outside.

It ran downstairs and into the living room, frightened the family who were there, and ran out. The owner went hysterical about the state of his home. So he phoned up HQ. The duty inspector came to the house. By this time, I said to Bob, 'You have to wait here until the boss sees you.' I apologised to the owners and went home. I completed a report and took it to HQ because I knew the chief constable would ask for one as soon as he was told about the complaint. There was a lot of fuss the next day, and I was sure this would be the end of Bob on the section. Bob turned up for work the next day, but there was no further action (NFA) on this incident. I will relay some more incidents involving Bob, and I doubt if you will believe any of them.

On one occasion, we were both in the dog van and going to HQ. The town centre had been altered to a one-way system, and a bus driver cut Bob up. So Bob, knowing the bus was going to the depot, raced down the one-way system and got ahead. He stopped the bus as it came into the terminus. He spoke to the driver and told him to secure the handbrake and stop the engine.

Bob boarded the bus, grabbed the driver, and headbutted the man so hard he fell unconscious on the floor. The passengers were shouting and yelling; the bus personnel went crazy. Bob just got back into the van, reversed up, and drove off to HQ, which was nearby. Another row started between Bob and me. I told him I would not back him up. That he was a bully and a coward and that all the time I have worked with him, I had not seen him arrest anyone his own size, who was not drunk, or a lot smaller. This infuriated him, and the HQ station officers pushed both of us through a gate into the charge room of the cell block, where I continued to shout at him and berated him. In the middle of this, half the population from the bus depot entered HQ and were all shouting and complaining about Bob.

The duty inspector came and told us to be quiet and to sit down. He asked me what was going on and if it was connected to the crowd in the station. Before I could speak, he left, and I told Bob, 'I am not getting involved. Give me the keys. You stay here and explain it to them.' I took the van, went to collect the meat for the dogs, and went home. Bob turned up later. I had fed the dogs, so we were done with work for the day. I had put the dogs away, and the van was garaged.

I told Bob, 'I don't want to be around you until I have heard from HQ.' HQ sent for me the next day, and it was the same duty inspector. We had words, and he told me no further action (NFA) was to be taken. So Bob walked away again. Everything I had achieved since taking on the section, all the success I had and the good relations and press reports, were being torn away.

People were frightened to call out a dog in case it was Bob who answered the call. On a lighter note, in the year and a half since I started, I had organised visits and lectures to schools with approval of the CC (chief constable). We had demonstrations at all schools, and the schools made us very welcome. The teachers included learned all about the section and the dogs.

My main objective was to educate the teenagers and anyone over ten years old, the age of criminal responsibility. The schools gave us good reports and asked if we could add a WPC to the visits to explain her work to the girl school leavers. We did, and the results were very pleasing. By this time, my dog was seven and a half years old. I took a six-month-old pup and worked the two dogs together.

The pup was a great floppy/furry animal. He kept falling over his great feet. He was not old enough to work, but he was a favourite in the younger children's classes. To introduce a bit of lighthearted fun, I taught the pup that when he heard the word *stand*, he would sit; when he heard the word *sit*, he had to lie down; and on a command to go down, he had to stand. When I entered a class, I told the pupils the pup was not yet a working dog, but he was learning the commands.

Elfie

Zak

I asked the pupils if they would like to see some obedience carried out by Elfie, my working dog. They unanimously said yes. I positioned Elfie in front of me nearest the children and the pup behind me, so I could not see him. Elfie was standing, so I gave her a command to sit. She sat quickly, but the pup heard the command, and he lay down. I would then command Elfie to lie down, and she would, but the pup would stand up.

All the pupils could see this, and they were giggling and raising their hands to tell me the pup was not doing it right. I would command Elfie to stand, and the whole class would laugh at the pup who had sat down. This took away the seriousness and broke the ice with the pupils. Most of them at some time would have been told, 'If you misbehave and are naughty, the policeman would come and take them away.'

I told them I had not ever taken children away, and if they needed help, it would be all right to speak to me outside of school. The head teacher wrote to the CC (chief constable) and praised the dogs and the officers for spending time at their school. On one occasion, I could not attend, so Bob had to go do the talk and demonstrate the dog's obedience.

The teachers brought in all the pupils, and they all sat round the outside edges of the assembly hall and had placed a wooden vaulting horse in the centre for the dog to jump over. Bob had not given the dog a chance to clean out before he went into the hall. The dog was disobedient, and Bob started shouting at it. This frightened the children. He commanded the dog to jump over the vaulting horse, which it did, and then it squatted down and unloaded poo everywhere.

Bob ended up shouting at the dog, which ran past him and outside, where it unloaded again. The school hall stunk, and the caretaker had to clean up the mess. My house phone rang, and I went out. I knew it would be HQ after the school complained. Bob was summoned to HQ to explain what had taken place. The result was the same NFA (no further action).

In one visit to the school, he had undone all the work I had been doing for over two years. My position was becoming untenable. I submitted reports to HQ trying to justify the dog section, but no changes were made. Rows between Bob and I were happening on a daily basis. I changed my shifts and kept apart from Bob as much as I could. Officers from other forces began to miss training days because of Bob.

Middlesbrough, Newcastle, North Yorkshire, Cumberland, and Northumberland were all concerned about the disruption this man was causing and were changing their training days to avoid Bob. Time moved on, and during a hot summer day, the officers training had lunch in a pub. When they resumed training and went to their vehicles, two dogs were found dead in a van.

You can only imagine the trouble this caused. Senior officers called meetings to review the situation. As I was not on that particular training day, I was sent to the meetings to represent Gateshead. The end result from my senior officers was again NFA (no further action) but to continue as before.

On one occasion, when I was on duty one Saturday and Bob was on a day off, Bob turned up in uniform, put his dog in the van, and told me he had been called to the training school, so I drove to Crook. As we passed through the village, Bob asked me to call at a shop where he would get some cigs. He went to Lipton's shop, and while he was inside, I changed the radio to receive messages on the county band and could hear their HQ.

Bob came back and said, 'Let's go.' It was about five miles to the school, and messages started to come through, asking for any car in the Crook area to respond. I could not respond because this trip was not officially reported to our own HQ. We arrived at the school Bob said he would be about thirty minutes and went into the school. I drove around to the kennels and went into the office to see the kennel boss, Kevin.

He was in the office with other officers, and they were monitoring the radio to see what was developing in Crook village. I exchanged greetings and had a cup of tea with them. Kevin had a lot of questions for me about Bob. It transpired from the radio messages that someone had entered a store, gone into the manager's office, and beat him up so much that an ambulance had been called and had taken him to the hospital.

Kevin took me to one side and told me the man who had been assaulted was the partner of Bob's girlfriend. He was an alcoholic and had been with her for years. But he was the manager at Lipton's store. At this point, the realisation of what was going on dawned on me. I drank my tea and went back to the van and waited, and eventually, Bob returned.

He was his normal self and said, 'Let's go back now.' I confronted Bob with what was going on, and he just said, 'It's sorted. We can go now.' I questioned him about what he had dragged me into—a domestic row between his girlfriend and partner, an assault on the guy in his shop, criminal damage, lies, lies, lies. I deliberately drove down Crook High Street, but there was no activity going on.

All the police had gone. Had they still been there, I would have told them about visiting the shop. Bob could take his chances. I argued with Bob all the way back to Gateshead. I even threatened to arrest him. I left him in the van at home and went indoors. I went into the sub-office, and I wrote a statement with all the details of what had taken place. I made two copies, which I placed in my lockable filing cabinet.

Then I made up my pocketbook, and the entry read, 'Visit training school', covering my back again. After that, it was routine as normal. In the next couple of days, I was off duty. The training school had contacted HQ because the van had been seen in Crook, and because Bob was on duty, he had been called into the office. I can't even begin to guess what he had said, but I was called to HQ urgently and directed to the chief superintendent's office.

Upon arrival at HQ, I was met by the duty inspector who was white and shaking. He took me straight to the superintendent's office. I could hear a dog barking as we got nearer; I could hear shouting. I opened the door and was confronted with the sight of Bob's dog pinning the boss against the wall. The dog was on his hind legs and had one front leg on each of the walls in the corner, trapping the chief superintendent. The dog was going crazy. The boss was screaming obscenities at me. It was obvious the dog was out of control, and instructions would have been futile. So I walked behind the dog and did what needed to be done. He turned on me and flew at me. I had to take desperate measures to regain control. I grabbed him in an armlock around his neck and held him until the boss escaped.

I was trying to calm the dog down, and I remembered what Kevin had told me to do when a dog was truly out of control. So I took hold of his ear and sunk my teeth in so hard the barking turned to a whimpering. The dog then lay on the floor, legs up. He could now hear commands, and I told him to stay. His lead was on the desk, so I reached for it and slipped it on him.

I kept the lead short and quietened the dog right down. I was able to lead the dog out. As I went, I noticed all the floor in the corner was wet. The boss must have peed himself. I took the dog outside and put him in the kennel where we kept strays. I returned to the front office and was told to find Bob and get him back there pronto. I gathered from the PCs in the station that Bob had been sent for and had a blazing row with the chief superintendent, so much so he had put his appointments (i.e. handcuffs, truchen and whistle, warrant card) on the desk and told the boss to stick his job up his backside. He had gone out and returned with the dog and said, 'You can keep your dog as well.' And he took its lead off and set the dog on the boss. It was probably the only time it took any notice of instruction.

I left instructions that when Bob was located, he had his dog to bring home. I went home and talked to Jenn. It was clear the bush telegraph was working well. Betty next door had been told by her hubby who was at HQ all day what had been going on at the station, and she in turn told Jenn, so I just filled in the blanks. Jenn and I discussed the event and wondered if this would be the end for Bob.

We also talked about where my future was going, and I could see no way forward as long as Bob was involved. One of the inspectors from Durham County Force had taken an appointment at Tyne Tees TV Studios. The programme was a forerunner to crime watch. Then he retired from the force and was employed full time at the TV studios. He took over security of all the TV buildings and vehicles/equipment.

He was upgrading the old British Legion men doing security work and replacing them with younger men. I spoke to him on the phone and arranged an interview. During which I outlined all the problems I had at work, and I was looking for a change. After two more interviews, I went to the studios, and he gave me some news. He told me that Gateshead Police were to be taken over by Durham County Police.

The merger would take place in September; it was now July. He also told me that my personal collar number would become 2007, which, in itself, would bring hassle from the villains. He said if I talked it over with Jenn, he would give me a job at the studios as a security officer. This merger had not been mentioned at all at work. Nobody had heard about it.

Jenn and I looked at this long and hard. If I took up this job, it meant a house move, school changes, etc. On the plus side, it would mean more money. I went to the council and enquired about getting a house. I was told I could have one on the developing estate where I lived. Jenn said I was not happy and getting into more trouble with the dogs; she would be happy if we moved.

A few more incidents and clashes with Bob and his mad dog pushed me a little more towards leaving. If I stayed, the merger would swallow up the dog section, and our two handlers would be brought into line with their section, which would mean £12 loss per week for me. Jenn would rather I left because of all the violence we got involved in with the dogs. I did not mention anything to Bob about me considering leaving.

Together with Jenn, I had written out my notice to leave but had not handed it in yet. It was now August. As usual, Sod's law intervened in the form of incidents at work. A popular hotel in town called the Five Bridges had the whole ground floor designed as a ten-pin bowling alley and was very well used. They had fifteen bowling lanes, a cafe, a bar, changing rooms, and a locker area. I was at home, and a call came to turn out both dogs and go to the hotel. Some kind of dispute with staff and bowling alley drunks.

On my arrival, a couple of traffic and beat officers were trying to control a crowd. I looked at the situation and instructed the officers to get the staff off the floor and close the cafe/bar and open the main front doors. I took Bob and both dogs into the bowling alley. There were people fighting everywhere, between 150–200 people, completely out of hand.

Bob and I took the dogs to the far end of the hall and started shepherding people toward the front door. People were throwing bowling balls, skittles, and anything else they could find. My training lead had clips on each end; with one end on the dog and the other end clipped to my wristband, it gave me a radius of ten feet all around me and still left me hands-free.

The noise and chaos was so bad that people started running to the front doors. Anyone who came within my protection area was bitten. As Bob and I swept everyone to the front exit and on to the streets, more reinforcements were arriving and controlling the crowds leaving the alley. It took about five to ten minutes, and everyone was outside somewhere being treated by paramedics for the dog bites.

I instructed Bob to put his dog in the van, and mine was laying down in the locker area. She was quiet and cleaning herself of blood. Once the hall and streets were cleared, the staff were allowed back into the alley. My dog was in the locker area. Somehow, some drunk had slipped past me and into the locker area behind me. He made his way towards the dog.

He bent down in front of the dog's face and barked at it. The end result was, paramedics took him to the hospital. The dog had only one bite, but the damage was 180 stitches in his face and neck, together with a dislocated lower jaw. The incident helped me make up my mind to hand in my notice. Of course, I discussed this with Jenn and said, 'I was so sick and tired of all the violence, and I was worried in case someone got really hurt.'

Training day

In the days leading up to me leaving the force, I continued to train my dogs. It was at the rugby club ground in Gateshead. The club allowed us use of their facilities. I was on the field when Bob turned up with his dog. I was searching a marked-out area for small articles. Bob brought his dog and walked right through the search area.

I remonstrated with him, but his attitude was, 'You're leaving, and that puts me in charge of the section, so don't even think about telling me what to do ever again.' I wanted to smack him, but I only had two days before I finished. I did not want to leave on a bad note, so I just walked away. He did a couple of simple exercises, but then his dog did the unmentionable thing and ran after a small dog that had got into the club grounds.

He shouted commands for the dog to return, but his dog ignored him. It chased the small dog into some undergrowth where it could not follow, and Bob had to go and get it. He brought it back up the field and was ill-treating it all the way. He arrived beside me, and his dog was still playing up, so much so it turned on him, snarling/growling. He pulled the lead tight and started to swing the dog round.

It was so severe that the dog left the ground. He swung it two or three times, passing the lead over his head. Then he moved towards a nearby tree and smacked the dog into the trunk. The dog's body wrapped around the tree with a sickening crack, and it fell to the ground and just lay there. I put my dog in the down position, slipped the choke chain off, and made a large loop. I ran past Bob and slipped my chain over his head and, at the same time, threw my lead over a low branch.

I had also deliberately ran into Bob, sending him sprawling on hands and knees. This gave me enough time to grab my lead and yank it. Bob stood up, and I pulled him up until his feet were just nearly touching the ground. He was gagging and clutching at the chain. I wanted the red mist to come down so I could really lay into him. However, I satisfied myself by smacking him in a few downward blows with the heel of my open hand on to the bridge of his nose.

There was blood everywhere. I knew the result would be two black eyes. He would have to explain. I released him and left the field. He was bleeding profusely, coughing and swearing. I said to him, 'You're in charge. Sort this out.' And I left him to it. I did not see him for a couple of days, by which time he looked like a panda with great big black eyes. Strangely, he did not speak to me. I continued to live next door to him for a year. His family avoided me when possible.

September came, and I put my letter of resignation in. My boss just said, 'Yes, just leave it in the in tray. Goodbye.' Not the reaction I thought would happen. I took up my new job, but when I went to the council to pick up my keys, I was told it had been decided not to allow me a council house because I had virtually made myself homeless, and I would have to go to the bottom of the allocation list for a house.

After one month, Durham County Force sent me a letter telling me I had to vacate my house ASAP, as it was wanted for the next dog handler. I spoke to my new boss, and he said, 'Do what you can, if anything, to move. Durham Police would take about two months before they would send you notices to quit.'

There was more worry for Jenn and the kids. Eventually, the notices to get out came and gave my dates when the police would evict me and remove my belongings. It was Wednesday, 2 p.m. I told my boss at TV studios. He said, 'Don't worry. It won't come to that. I will take care of you.' He came to me on the Monday prior to the eviction on Wednesday and said, 'Take Wednesday off. Stay at home. I will come to your home Wednesday morning. Tell your lady wife not to worry.'

Wednesday came, and about eight, a whole broadcast team arrived outside. They set up TV cameras on the substation office, the car park, and my home. Lighting and speaker systems were set up. At one thirty, they cleared an area in the car park and set up cameras, speakers, microphones—the whole works for an interview. Newscasters and makeup girls, the works. At two, two official cars, followed by a furniture removal van and police officers in overalls arrived. The official cars had a senior officer with paperwork. He got out of his car and stood a few minutes taking in all the TV equipment and personnel.

He eventually decided to get back into his car, and all the police left. They did not even knock at my door. Within one hour, the whole TV staff and equipment were dismantled and gone back to the studio. My boss told me that when I eventually leave, there would be a rent bill to pay. He had enquired what that would be, and I put it away each month. I remained in that house exactly one year before I moved.

While I was still in the force, one of the traffic drivers asked if I could do him a favour with the van. He had been given a large beer barrel by a publican. He was going to cut it in half and varnish it, then place the two halves in his garden for decoration filled with flowers. We measured the van cages, and the barrel would go in one side and the two dogs in the other. I arranged to pick up the barrel on the following Thursday, and if my friendly driver was busy, I would drop the barrel in his garden.

This was the only time the publican could be there to help. Everything went okay. I picked up the barrel and was en route to drop it off. Sod's law intervened, and the dogs were needed to attend a scene of crime. So it was blue lights and two tones back across town. It was an urgent request. As I made my way, the dogs were stirring restless, noisy, and excited.

I was almost there, and HQ, via the radio, cancelled my attendance. I switched off the two tones and blue lights and conformed to the speed limit of thirty miles per hour. There was so much noise, and I could smell ale. It was getting stronger, and I could hear the dogs lapping something. The barrel had fallen over, and the contents of twenty-year-old hops and barley were slopping about on the floor.

The dogs were drinking this and slurping it down. I eventually arrived, and as it was in the middle of a steep street, the hops and liquid were leaking out under the doors. I made the mistake of opening both doors. The barrel came out of one side, and the hops and slops cascaded out the other side. My trousers from the knees down plus my shoes were soaked and stinking of stale ale.

I got the barrel into a place in the garden. The dogs had come out like they were on a water slide and had shot down the hill about thirty-plus meters. They could not stand up, and I thought it was because of the gunge they were covered in. When I got to them, I realised that they were paralytic drunk. They could not stand because their legs turned into rubber.

The only way to get them back into the van was to slip a lead on and drag them one at a time back to the van. I eventually recovered both of them. On the way home, they went to sleep on their backs, legs akimbo. Jenn was at home, so I left the van in the car park and went to get her. I just asked if she could help. Her friend Betty was with her, so they both came to have a look. They went to the van and looked in.

The stink was overpowering, and it took a few seconds for the vision to sink in and realise. The dogs were drunk to the point of passing out. They helped get the dogs into the kennels, and I connected a hose so I could wash the van out and get rid of the smell. The girls were in hysterics; they each had a dog on a lead and were imitating me training, giving the dogs commands. The dogs were trying to stand, but their legs were like a newborn giraffe. They wobbled every which way and were limp. I hosed the dogs down and got rid of all the hops and gunge. The girls were still hysterical and went indoors only to emerge with bath towels and hair dryers together, with a huge bag of curlers.

I put the dogs inside the kennel instead of the outside runs. This was to stop prying eyes of the public and Bob. The dogs had hangovers for three days. It was terrible. I was able to avoid call-outs and jobs for the dogs. I said they had a bug and were not well, so they eventually came back to the land of the living on the fourth day. I cancelled a school trip and rearranged for another date.

The news of the paralytic dogs leaked out, and I was receiving leaflets for the Alcoholics Anonymous for dogs. Many jokes and cartoons kept coming. None of the bosses mentioned the incident.

There was another incident later on. Everyone told me to keep it quiet. Our friends had got tickets for a mediaeval feast at a castle. Waiting time for a booking was well over a year. On the date of the feast, Jenn and our family were still living in the police house. The coach came, and everyone on it were policemen of various ranks, including an inspector—Paddy 'Fag Ash' McDonald.

He sat in the first seat as you entered the coach. He made some remarks as we boarded, but Jenn just pushed me into the bus. I did not hear the remark, but Jenn just steered me to a seat in the back row. For Jenn and me, it was a fabulous night. There were 350 people sitting at long tables in the great hall. All the staff in period dress, seven-course meal. Each place had one dagger sticking in the table and two plates— i.e. one dinner plate and one side plate.

As each course was being served, the first serving went to the king's taster. He would, via microphone, tell you how to eat whatever it was. There were jesters, jugglers, and acrobats. The entertainment was non-stop. The only drinks available were lager in a tankard or mead in a small glass bigger than a shot glass. Jenn could not drink the larger, so she tried the mead.

It was a sweet honey mead, and she liked it. The serving girls kept topping up everyone's glasses, so we all lost track of how much we drank. The guy opposite Betty was pulling a chicken apart with his hands; he tore a leg off and lost his grip. The chicken flew over the table and hit Betty in the neck area. It was dripping in grease and slid down to rest on her low-cut dress.

One of the girls led Betty away, got her cleaned up, and gave her a waitress's blouse to wear. So the night went on getting noisier and funnier. People were dancing between the tables. The same guy involved with the chicken tripped, and a full pint of lager went all over Betty. Again, staff came to the rescue and sorted her out. The evening was ending, and people were leaving.

We all headed for our coach, except Jenn and Betty. It had been snowing while we were indoors. So Jenn and Betty started a snowball war in the car park. They were pleasantly drunk and enjoying themselves. We eventually went to get on the bus. Who better to greet us than Paddy 'Fag Ash' McDonald. As Jenn got on the bus and went up the stairs, she came face to face with Paddy. He made some derogatory remarks and then reeled back, squealing in pain. He passed out. Jenn had unleased a left jab immediately followed by a right hook.

Then she just went up the bus to the back, singing and dancing with all the passengers. Nobody was aware of what had happened at that point. The bus left, and there was a problem. At the front, Paddy had come to and was throwing his rank and his weight about in the form of complaints to the driver. By this time, the mead and the cold air had really got to Jenn.

She was drunk. Paddy sent another PC to have words with Jenn. He had to get close to make himself heard. By then, Jenn was really out of it. She threw up all over this fellow, and he was in a hell of a mess. The driver did not stop until we were back at HQ. We got Jenn and Betty home. Jenn was picking up again and started singing. Eventually, we settled and went to bed.

At about dinner time next day, an official car arrived in our car park, and two officers got out. One came across and knocked on the door. Then he went back to his car to help his mate. They delivered the biggest bunch of flowers I had ever seen, and they said they were from everyone on the bus for Jenn, and so ended our night at the castle. As I was no longer in the force, it was business as usual. No further action.

My two aunts Anne and Hilda were now seventy-seven years old and decided to go to Australia to visit Meg, their sister. They were well aware of my situation with the police house. They talked with Jenn and I and asked if Jenn would take over the shop and keep it in the family. They would also help us get a house of our own by paying a deposit on a new house.

We said yes. Jenn changed her job and worked in the shop with Hilda. We bought/put a deposit on a four-bedroom house at a place about five miles out of town. It meant the kids would stay at school where they were. Jenn would drive into town and drop the kids at my mother's, and they would go to school from there or have their tea with Grandma. Jenn would bring them home.

When I left the force at Gateshead, I became a security officer for Tyne Tees Television Studios Channel 8 in Newcastle upon Tyne. The firm employed hundreds of staff and tradespeople. There was a complex of buildings to accommodate all these people. Joiners, plumbers, electricians, painters, hairdressers, makeup department, office staff, and restaurant staff were all housed in the complex in 480 offices.

I was on a late shift, two to ten. On most days, all the employees had left by 6 p.m., except for the ten o'clock newsreader; he would be in the news room until 10.30 p.m. The night-duty security man would arrive about 9.45 p.m. At 7 p.m., I would go round the building and lock all ground floor doors on the outside of the buildings and return to the reception in case there were any stragglers. They would know the only way out was via the reception.

On this occasion, a young joiner had asked his boss if he could work late. He was making a dining room set for himself. At 9 p.m., I heard the lift start up. The doors to the lifts were to my left, and from my desk, I looked across to see who was coming. The doors opened, and the young joiner stepped out. He was holding his arms across his chest, and his hands where under his armpits. It was obvious he was in trouble. He stumbled forward a couple of steps and asked for help before he passed out.

I could see his hands now, and he only had his thumbs left on each hand. All the other fingers were missing. He was bleeding heavily. There were bandages in the first-aid box. I took a couple and tied them tightly around his wrists. This was only temporary to stem the flow of blood. I moved him to a sitting position next to a chair and raised his arms up as high as possible.

The lad came around and was now conscious. I told him to hold his arms up. I also had time to enter an adjoining room where I could get clean towels and tea cloths. I also phoned the newsreader and told him to call an ambulance to come to the reception because a joiner had been in an accident. I returned to the lad and checked the bandages.

I also used the towels to wrap his hands up. He had regained a bit of colour. I told him there was an ambulance en route. The newsreader turned up, and I asked him to stay with the lad while I went into the joiners shop. I took my sandwich box and went to recover the missing fingers. They were easily found, so I switched off the power to the machine and went into the lift to the top floor and collected some ice to preserve the fingers. Then I got back to the reception, the paramedics had arrived and were treating the lad.

They decided it would be best to take him in a sitting position, which they did. I gave the medics all the details of the lad, and they left. The newsreader returned to his post, and the night-duty security man arrived. I put him in the picture and gave him all the details of the joiner so his wife and boss could be told. I left for home.

Sometime later, I found out the lad's fingers had been stitched back on his hands, but he had only limited use of them, maybe 40 per cent.

On another occasion, while I was on duty in the reception—I had only just started and it was just after 2 p.m.—I was taking over the reception desk, and the early turn man was telling me who was who in the waiting area. There were lots of people milling about. Some were waiting to be collected from reception, some were wanting appointments, and some were waiting for taxis.

After about half an hour, the area had almost cleared. There were a couple of people waiting for secretaries to collect them and one visitor waiting for a taxi. I would like to explain. The reception had been refurbished and front entrance had been rebuilt into a glass frontage thirty feet wide and eighteen feet high, with only two doors in the centre built in a semicircle leading on to ten curved marble stairs down to pavement level. I was sitting at the desk when I saw a taxi pull up. It stopped to the right of the door, and a visitor who had been waiting got up and went in a direct line to the cab. This took him to the right of the doors, and he walked straight into the glass panel.

His right knee hit the glass, and the impact shattered the bottom two feet of glass, causing the man to fall with his right leg forward and his left leg twisted and backwards. The remainder of the glass slid down the frame like a French guillotine and cut the man's right upper leg to the bone. He was screaming, and blood was everywhere. Other people were starting to crowd the man. I asked one person to call an ambulance and two others to fetch towels from the room behind them.

All I could think about were first-aid rules—either remove the patient from the danger or remove the danger from the patient. I could see glass sticking in the wound, and it was broken away from the main glass, so I could move the patient back into the reception away from further danger. The patient himself pulled the broken glass out of his leg. I folded up a towel and placed it over the wound, then applied gentle pressure to keep the wound closed. As far as I could see, there was no damage to the arteries.

I raised the man's legs by his heels and placed them on a chair, and I got him to lean back with support. He was much calmer now. I told his taxi to go. The ambulance arrived and took over the patient, so I could organise the joinery department to get the window boarded up. I had talked to the patient, so I had his details to let his firm and his family know what had happened. The glass outside was taken away, and I called out a carpet cleaning company to clean up the reception carpet. The visitor went to the hospital, and some level of normality was achieved. I never heard from the visitor or saw him again; I can only presume he recovered.

I carried on at the TV company. The aunts sailed for Aussie, and I helped Jenn in the shop. We closed it for a week and completely refurbished it. We bought new fridges and new counters and made it semi-self-service. It was a great success, and Jenn and I worked long hours with the help of my mum. With my TV wages, we were well set up. I bought a new Ford Corsair for Jenn and a mobile shop which I would work. There are fourteen council estates around Gateshead.

I eventually left Tyne Tees and worked the mobile shop. I planned a route of all the estates and estimated how much time I could spend at each one. I took Mondays off to go to the cash and carry for stock. I also bought a pickup van for the cash-and-carry run. Money was coming in, and Jenn was able to pay back the aunts after one year. We decided to move back to Gateshead to save time travelling.

We sold the house and moved into town. The kids all changed school and went local to us. Life was looking up; we were making it good. But I lost the value of the pound in my pocket because I included all household bills with the cash and carry and paid them all. Jenn kept the books, and everything was well. We were considering buying ponies for the girls.

We had all the latest gear, furnishings, TVs, radiograms, carpets, everything at home. I had to put long hours working the shop, so I was up at 5 a.m. to get ready for my first stop at 8 a.m. I would work till 11 p.m. and be home by 12 p.m. Jenn would take care of the shop and kids together with everything else.

On my rounds, I began to notice a black car turning up at my selling places. It was easily recognisable as the Gateshead CID car occupied by two brothers, both detectives. Curiosity got the better of me, so I sneaked up on them and jumped in the back of the car. Once they got over the surprise and we exchanged greetings and pleasantries, they told me about someone committing robberies and wage snatches on a large scale.

I had been put in the frame. My past had come up—from squatting in a police house to opening a shop, plus acquiring a new house, new car, new mobile shop, and new mobile pickup. The twins had been allocated the job of watching me (surveillance). I told them I had paperwork and receipts for everything and invited them to come and check and search my home.

I also gave them a copy of my timetable, so they could get other jobs done and check on me at any point. They were with me for year and a half at different times and locations. Jenn said they could call at any time. Everything was up to date and filed, including all receipts, so it did not upset her. Monday was a busy day; it was cash-and-carry day to restock the mobile shop and the static shop.

Jenn and I were working in the rear store room at about eight. The shop was in darkness when we heard noises in the front shop. I switched off the light and told Jenn to keep quiet. We had three visitors in the front shop. They put the light on and went around filling their bags with groceries. Jenn and I watched until they were ready to leave.

We came into the shop and confronted these ladies who almost died of fright. We listened to them try to explain their actions, then Jenn switched on the till to tot up one of the bags, put all items through the till, and handed the receipt to each of them for all the groceries and everything else they had. Jenn told them she wanted the money from each of them by closing time tomorrow. I took from them the set of keys they had to the shop.

One of them was my aunt Maggie, and the others were her friends. Maggie told me they had been doing this for thirty years. Hilda and Annie knew all about it. I read the riot act to them and then showed them the door. They took all their purchases with them but came in and paid Jenn the next day. I changed the door locks in case there were any more relatives with keys. I also sacked all the sales reps who had been turning up for years. I could get all the goods they sold from cash and carry.

Life went on, and after a year and a half, the CID brothers told me that they had arrested somebody for all the robberies, so I was no longer a suspect. Just before Xmas, I took ill with fatigue, exhaustion, poleaxed. I tried to get another driver to help out, but no one came forward, not even my brother. I came off the road over Xmas, and when I picked up and went back to work, I was selling Xmas stock at Easter, and now I had to compete with three new supermarkets.

I could not match their prices. Even Jenn felt the backlash in her shop. We decided enough was enough. I found a buyer for the mobile shop. As it turned out, he also bought Jenn's shop, the pickup van, and all the stock. We decided Jenn would stay at home and take care of the family. I would find another job. We sold the house and moved back to town. I started work driving a bread-and-cake lorry. On my first day, I left my car in the car park, and it was stolen.

It had all my tools in the boot, together with Jenn's sheepskin coat, which was on the back seat. We never got it back. The job did not last. All the drivers and loaders were working a scam and splitting the money between them. I went bus driving for a while and then took a partnership with a friend hiring out building equipment, bulldozers, bobcats, JCBs, cement mixers, and much more.

Jenn could see I was not happy, and when I went home one night, she told me she had contacted a county council who was looking for a dog handler. She had arranged for the boss to meet me at a park in Newcastle for an interview. The only snag was, the job was with Chelmsford, Essex County Council. They had twelve parks, and vandalism repairs were costing a fortune. I had the interview and accepted the post. A house, uniform, van, and training course with a new dog were all part of the deal.

The boss would keep the job open for three months until Jenn and I visited Essex. I had no idea where Essex was apart from it being down south. Within the time limit, we moved to Essex, and the house was in a place called Chelmsford.

CHAPTER THREE

I duely did a course in Reading town, ran by a retired metropolitan dog handler. It really was a Mickey Mouse outfit, but I passed the course and started work alongside another handler. He had a nice dog but was spoiling it through his lack of knowledge. The job was good, and Jenn was happy. We enrolled the family into a comprehensive school, and they quickly made friends. I found the cost of living was very high, so to supplement, I took a second job as a taxi driver. The owner asked if I had a PSV licence and gave me a bus driving job on a few weekends. I soon learned the geography of the whole county through the taxi job.

When I checked up on the house, it was allocated to the prison service, and I could not be a council tenant in my own right for fifteen months. So things settled down, and the fifteen months passed. Jenn had made friends with neighbours and was pleased we were no longer in Gateshead. I came into contact with the local police during the summer. We spoke a lot about the police force, and I had learned that the force had been awarded several large pay raises since I left. I asked one of them to see what my pay scale would be if I rejoined.

Jenn and I had talked it through, and by going back into the force, I could treble my salary and cut my working time down to eight hours. We decided to go for it. I went on several interviews and accepted an offer of a job and its conditions on both sides. I was to reduce weight, which was no big problem, and on their part, they would not send me to a training school for three months. I could do a two-week course at

HQ, which was also in Chelmsford Town, and I would be posted to Chelmsford, so the children could remain at the comprehensive school.

The house was rented to me in my own right and not tied to any other departments. It was a great adventure for the whole family. Jenn and I loved it. The year was 1973; the girls were eleven and Derek now fourteen years old. The summers of '73, '74, and '75 were very hot. We had not seen this kind of summer in years. We all loved it. I promised myself the bad old bullying days were gone, and I would not upset the workers. On my first day at Chelmsford, known as Charlie Delta, I was taken to the parade room and introduced to the shift. There were twenty-eight men and a couple of WPCs. The shift sergeant was briefing the team and bringing them up to date with events. He also read out the jobs each had been allocated and sent them all out to get on with it, except me. He and I had a talk, and he said, 'I don't really know where to fit you in at the moment. The longest serving and most experienced PC on the station had four years' service behind him. Now you turn up with nearly nine years city service.'

I suggested, 'Why don't I take a radio and go and acquaint myself with the town centre, the beat PCs, and the various doormen and security men at different places?' The sergeant agreed. So off I went with no restrictions, a free hand. I did not mention my taxi and bus driving and knew the town like the back of my hand. The *A* shift operated two area cars, each with an experienced officer as an observer, Charlie Alpha One. One car covered the north of the town, and the other covered the south side. A week went by, and I asked the sergeant how I could get to drive a car.

He waited until the shift were all assembled and, taking the mickey out of me, told me that some of the shift had been waiting for a driving course for three years. And at the end of it, if they were assessed as drivers, they just *maybe* could get a job driving if someone leaves or is promoted.

I said, 'I have a permit. It was issued at Gateshead.'

His reply was, 'It will not be recognised here if you did not go through the driving school.' I spent the next couple of days freelancing in town.

Friday was my day off. So Jenn and I went to HQ driving school, and I asked to see the duty inspector. I was directed to his office, and Jenn waited in my car. I knocked on the door and was invited in. The inspector asked how he could help. I told him I was posted to Chelmsford Town and only had a permit issued at Gateshead. He asked me more questions and talked to me for a little while, then he rang a sergeant and asked him to bring a car around.

'The sergeant will give you a test run and let me know how you get on.' We had our run for about twenty-five minutes and returned. He told the inspector I was very good but a little rusty and recommended I be given a permit and an advanced course in six months' time. The inspector wrote out a permit and signed it there and then. Off I went to find Jenn, and she was delighted. We went out and had a meal to celebrate.

On the next shift parade, the sergeant was about to give out jobs. I said to him, 'Sergeant, those driving permits I asked about.'

He just smirked and said, 'Yeah, what about them?'

I said, 'Will this one do?' I slid it up the table to him. The looks on all the faces was a treat. The sergeant checked the permit and sent it back to me. He then altered the duty sheet and said, 'PC Waugh, driver you have Charlie Alpha One on the north side. Your observer is the usual driver of that car.' I left the station and had a good day. Many incidents came up in the next few months, and I dealt with more sudden deaths than ever before—industrial accidents, suicides, road traffic accidents, etc.

While on area car patrol, I was sent to help at the scene of an RTA. I could not get close to the wreckage because of the traffic being held up. I parked my car up and walked along the queue of traffic; there was no urgency as other officers were there.

As I walked past a huge articulated lorry in the queue, the driver opened his window and asked, 'Have you got a match, mate? I would like to smoke.'

I replied, 'It might be advisable to wait. There is a petrol tanker involved in the accident. You can smell petrol in the air.'

I got to the junction where the wreckage was. I was asked to assist in moving traffic on and making way for recovery vehicles to get near. I started clearing the main road queue, and I could guide vehicles past the wreckage. In a short time, I was able to move cars on the road. I walked in on a dozen or more cars cleared, and the next one was the lorry where I spoke to the driver. He was not moving no matter how I waved at him, so I walked back to the lorry, and I could see the driver with his head tilted forward. I got right to the lorry and opened the driver's door, which was higher up than me.

I was greeted by a horrendous sight of blood, skin, and intestines. The smell was terrible. The lorry's load of scaffolding poles had moved and had shot forward through the rear of the cab, through the back of his driving seat, through his body, and out to the front of the cab. I checked his wrist for a pulse but could not find one. So I stepped up higher so I could check his neck arteries. There was no vital signs; the driver was dead. I was joined by other traffic officers who had come to find out what the holdup was. We cordoned off the vehicle and called out the doctor to certify the death of the driver. We now had a second incident to deal with.

The traffic officers checked over the load. The poles had been loaded longways on the lorry and formed a pyramid as they got higher; they were secured by chains which were intact and secured properly. Only a small section had slid forward when the driver braked to join the queue of traffic. I was told to return to my station and have a break. The driver was removed from the cab and poles and then taken to the morgue.

I have been reminded of an incident at Gateshead in my early days. I took a driving course and was given a permit. Often I was asked to take out a panda (mini police car) and complete my shift with it. I was driving through an industrial area estate which was very big. At the end of the estate, it bordered with Durham County, and a massive area was a railway shunting yard and sidings.

As I was going to be off my patch, my options were to turn around and go back or to go through the shunting yard for half a mile. And this would bring me out near the A1 route, which was in my area. I chose the road through the shunting yard. Eleven bridges crossed this road, and all of them pretty close to each other. Railway stock was being moved on dozens of lines above me. It only took a couple of minutes to reach the A1 safely.

I turned and headed into town. I heard and felt an almighty bang; it shook the ground beneath me. The noise of screeching metal was over very quickly. The radio called for any car near the shunting yard. I responded and returned the way I came. I turned on to the road through the yard and could see clouds of dust rising above the first bridge. The centre trucks had derailed and slid down the embankments and piled up in a heap, which totally covered the road up to the bridge.

The forward trucks were still on the line and linked to the rest. The last six trucks were still on the line and linked to the wreckage of the centre trucks. After I returned to the bridge and saw the train derailment, I spoke to BR engineers. I told them I had just passed under this bridge a few minutes ago. They said they would deal with it, as no one was hurt and told me how lucky I was not to have been under the pile of waggons.

I left the area, and on the way home, I stopped, opened the door, and stood up outside. At that point, I felt so ill. I projectile-vomited and coughed, choked, and coughed again. When the vomiting stopped, I realised my bowels had blown and emitted into my trousers (diarrhoea and urine). What a state I was in! Feeling awful, I just got back into the mini and sat for a moment. The smell was the next to hit me. So I drove off and went home. Because I was in such a bad state, I did not want to be stopped or seen by anyone, and I went off my patch. I drove via the back streets. Eventually, I got home and entered my yard via the rear door.

I could see Jenn through the window and quickly told her what had happened. She said, 'Stay there. Don't come in. Take your clothes off.' As it was a small enclosed yard, I started to strip. Jenn connected a small hose to the sink tap and said, 'When you are ready.' I piled my gear up in the corner. Jenn turned the tap on, and I hosed myself down. Jenn said she would get me hot water to finish rinsing me down, together with a towel.

I dried myself, and Jenn was putting my clothes into a plastic bag. I went indoors to get clean clothes from upstairs. As I went through the house naked, I went through the living room, I was nearly through before I realised my mother-in-law and two sisters-in-law were in there. They cheered and laughed whilst making remarks. I just carried on through and went upstairs. It was totally embarrassing for me, but I could see the funny side of it.

With clean uniform on, I had to get to the station to fill up with petrol. That was to be my excuse for being off my beat. While at the station, I went to the uniform stores and collected a new uniform, two shirts, and socks to replace the dirty gear, which I would burn later in the metal bin. I returned to my beat and felt okay now that I was dry and clean, and I made sure the car was clean inside and out, but I was hungry.

When I finished my shift and went home. Jenn had told the family to go home and had made me a lovely dinner. I told her my sad, sorry story, and we turned it into a joke and had a good laugh. My sisters-in-law and mother-in-law took the mickey when I saw them later. So it was just another day at the office.

There was another occasion when I was called to a sudden death. Then when I arrived, I was shown into a back bedroom. A doctor had been and certified the death, and the undertaker's men were about to remove the body. It was an old man lying in bed. He had been lying on a live electric blanket for about three weeks, and where the blanket touched his skin, it was bubbling like something simmering in the pan. He had several cats, which had been eating his flesh. The smell was terrible.

The undertaker decided to leave the man on the mattress, so they took the two corners at the head and toe and simply folded it around the body and lifted the whole thing into a metal coffin to take it to the morgue. The old gent lived alone, had no known relatives, and died all alone. These facts have haunted me for a lifetime. I got back into my transport, and I felt itchy and could see insects on my clothes. I realised I was covered in fleas. I went home, and it was a repeat of strip off in the yard.

I put my clothes in the bin after emptying my pockets and burnt the whole lot. I told Jenn not to come out and just poke the hose through the window, and after a washdown, I would need clean gear. I burnt all my old infested uniform and shirt and underwear. All I could think of was, *Don't let these fleas get indoors amongst my three children.* Luckily, none did come indoors. The house where the old man lived was fumigated and cleaned.

Being a driver brought niggles with it because at the start of a shift, I would examine my car for marks, dents, scrapes, and damages. I was the one who signed for the car to say none of the above had been found, and it would be my permit removed if I did not report anything and then found it halfway into a shift. Also, as a personal thing to me, if I did not have any pressing enquires, I would take the car to HQ and put it through the car wash. I hated driving a dirty car.

I also submitted a report requesting that the experienced officers stop being deployed as observers and suggested they be replaced by recruits. This way, the recruits or cadets could gain a wider variety of offences to deal with. Also, they would meet other officers who had their own rural beats and see more of the county. The inspector implemented this suggestion, and so recruits or cadets became observers. Everyone seemed pleased.

It also gave drivers the chance to play tricks on the recruits and teach them and keep them alert. On night shift, it would become almost impossible for recruits to remain awake, especially after the tea break. I got together with the other driver and arranged to meet him at Hylands Park's main entrance. If his observer went to sleep by 3 a.m. and my observer also, I would creep quietly along to the park, and there, I would swap places and cars with the other driver.

We left there and waited for the observers to wake up. Some just kept quiet; others wanted to know what was going on. And we could tell them anything, to make out they had slept through something exciting. Eventually, we would meet up and take back our own cars and warn the recruits to say nothing. Sometimes we got a really obnoxious recruit, so after break on nights, when he dropped off to sleep, I would go to Writtle Village and drive into the pond at the edge with the recruit in the deepest part. I would stop the car, lean over the recruit, and open his door off the lock. I would switch on the blues and twos, shake the recruit, and shout at him to get out. He would stumble out into the water, fall over, and get soaked.

I would close his door and leave him in the lake, then drive off and switch off the blues and twos, leaving the recruit to find his own way back to the nick. It usually took about an hour. If I got a shout from HQ, I would pick up the recruit and attend whatever HQ wanted. Very rarely after that did any of the recruits sleep on my watch. Some of the recruits had no idea how to approach members of the public, even less idea on how to tell them they have committed an offence and would be reported for it or how to caution the suspect and note his/her reply. In view of this, I spoke to each recruit and told them from now on they would listen to me 'caution and charge offenders with whatever offence', and then they would do the same with the next offender. This worked well, and it made the recruits check that the offences were made clear. It also gave them a chance to go to court and learn the procedure for the courtroom.

So I began to keep a ledger in the car and recorded every offence the recruits dealt with, full details of everything that took place, and what was said. Each recruit had their own allocated pages, and I got them to keep the entries up to date with court dates and results of cases. This created a lot of interest for these young officers and made them feel they were trusted and involved in the work. I would check regularly that their paperwork was up to date and submitted on time.

Generally, keep an eye on them, and keep them busy. Of course, all this took time, and I found I was putting in less paperwork. After a couple of months, on an average shift, a driver could do between six to ten pieces of paperwork and clock up between 150–200 miles a shift. Eventually, I was summoned to the inspector's office; it was for an assessment of my work, bearing in mind I was also a probationary officer at this stage. I pulled into CID and parked up. I took my recruit into the station and told her to get her paperwork and pocketbook up to date and wait in the parade room for me.

I went into the inspector's office, and he had the sergeant in with him. He preambled and went over various events I had attended. Overall, he was generally satisfied with my progress and how I had settled in with the shift members, but he said my work had dropped off in the last couple of months, and he hoped I was not one of the lazy officers who, after settling in, would not bother too much. I stopped him in mid flow and asked, 'Could I bring something from the car which might explain things for both of you?' I left the office and returned with my recruit ledger. I explained that since recruits were allowed to be observers, they should be busy.

I showed them the ledger and how it was divided up to suit the recruits. Each had their own section and kept it up to date with their pocketbooks, notes, and reports that had been submitted and on the results of the court cases. He was very curious and interested in this book. He said I should return to patrol and asked if I would leave the ledger with him. I could collect it before going off duty. The shift was only an hour to go, so I took the recruit to HQ, washed, and fuelled the car, ready for the handover at the end of the shift.

I saw my sergeant, and he told me to pick up my ledger at the next shift. The boss was going through it. Sure enough, I got it in the shift parade room, but not before we got a lecture that all drivers would adopt my system for the observers. He gave every driver a ledger and explained how he wanted everything recorded and cases followed through to conclusion at court. He never mentioned my book or what had been said by the boss, and so my system came into being.

My feeling good only lasted a few days until I dealt with an incident at Galleywood—a sudden death. Warning: not for the faint-hearted. Before you read any further, the next part has graphic descriptions in which it may shock you, and disgust you. It will certainly surprise and amuse most of you.

The radio sounded, 'Charlie Alpha One, attend sudden death at the caravan site at Galleywood.'

My response was, 'CA 1 10-4.' At the time of this message, I was parked in the High Street. My WPC recruit had popped into the chemist. I was answering the radio when she came to the car. She threw a paper bag on the bonnet and announced she would be back in a moment. The contents of the bag slid out down the bonnet. The WPC disappeared into a shop. Members of the public were making remarks and laughing. The contents were sanitary towels, and the engine vibrating was making them slide down the bonnet.

I switched on the two tones, and the WPC came back, picked up her shopping, and got in. I shot off for Galleywood. As it was not an emergency, I switched of the two tones. I explained we were going to a sudden death and told her, 'There is only three forms to fill in, and we have to call the coroner's officer after we have checked the body, to make sure no foul play has taken place. It is also required we don't disturb the scene in case it's a suicide. Check for pills or poisons nearby.'

The WPC said, 'I have never seen a dead person before.' So I talked to her and suggested she stay out of the caravan until I have checked the body and the place over.

'If everything is straightforward, I will come and get you and come back in with you.'

She said, 'Yes.'

'Members of other caravans found this chap and will be there. Also, there may be relatives present. Say as little as possible and preserve as much dignity as possible.'

We arrived on the scene, and there were two ladies outside the caravan. I asked, 'Did you find the body, and are you related? Give your details to my colleague.'

While I checked the caravan, one lady said, 'I put the blanket on him. I don't want it back.' I stepped into the van. The smell was terrible. When a person passes away, certain things take place within the body, i.e. the bowels will empty out, urine will flow until the bladder is empty, and it is possible to have a rush of blood to parts of the body, which will enlarge them. In this case, it was an old man who was wearing only a T-shirt.

He was sitting in his chair, leaning forward. I removed the blanket and saw the old man's hands around his penis—both hands, one on top of the other. By the size, it was obvious he must have been masturbating, and the final rush of blood had greatly enlarged his penis, before rigor mortis set in. This causes the whole body to freeze like a statue and will remain so for a few hours. There were no signs of foul play there. I lifted the blanket up and covered the old man's body to the shoulders. The expression on his face was classic—face screwed up, eyes shut.

My own thoughts were, *He masturbated until ejaculation and brought on a heart attack.* His bowels emptied, but he stayed in the same position. *Ding!* An evil idea formed. My recruit had not seen the body. I went out spoke to my WPC and told her it was a straightforward death, no foul play. If she wanted to, she could go in and check him out. She said she wanted to; it was the only way to learn. She went in, stopped at the door, and gagged at the smell.

I said, 'If you're okay, go ahead, walk round him. If you're ready, remove the blanket.' She gagged again and was feeling sick. I said, 'Remove the blanket.' She did. She gagged and threw up/screamed, and in her rush to get out, she fell into the mess on the floor. I asked, 'Can I help you?' She was screaming hysterically. The two women tried to help her, but she screamed abuse at them and ran off down the road and off the caravan site. The coroner's officer turned up, and the undertakers removed the body to the chapel of rest. I got a signature in my pocketbook to say I had handed the body to the undertaker.

My job was done here. The site owner took charge of the caravan. I drove to the local office at Galleywood and rang my sergeant. He came on the phone and just laughed. I asked, 'Is my observer there?'

He said, 'She was in the boss's office, in a hysterical fit, and it was all your fault.'

I thought, *There goes my brownie points.*

The sergeant said, 'Give it an hour before you come in.' After one hour, I went in and into the boss's office. He was trying to be serious and pointed out that as a senior officer, I had a duty of care towards recruits. He really could not look at me, and he kept the lecture going. I coughed. He thought I was laughing, and he could not continue his lecture. He just burst out laughing.

He said, 'You could have done it differently. God only knows if she will ever get over the trauma.' He had to call in the force doctor and her parents to take her home.

I asked, 'Have you seen her?'

He replied, 'No. She ran all the way here in that state.'

I replied, 'At least she's fit.'

He just said, 'Get back to work. No more nonsense.'

I left his office and met head-on coming down the corridor my sergeant, WPC, and her parents (Sod's law). I asked the WPC if she was ready to finish her shift.

The sergeant opened an office door beside me and pushed me in, then he escorted his party off the premises. I left the building via the downstairs garage door and continued my shift. If you have any kind of imagination, you can envisage my in tray filling up with cartoon drawings, memos, pictures, and suggestions from everyone.

On another occasion, I was sent to investigate a suicide on the main railway line through CD. I arrived at the location and was met by an ambulance crew who had located a body of a man on the line.

The body was headless, and they could not locate the head. I said we would go and search the line from where the body was located. Before we started the search, I returned to my car and collected a towel from my personal bag of spare clothing, and we started the search in the same direction as the train had been travelling, one on either side of the line, after we had assurance from the railway police that no more trains were due.

We started walking alongside the track, searching the area as we went. After a good search of the area, we had covered about 100 yards from the body. The greenery and foliage on the side of the track thinned out, and I could see something that did not fit in with the surrounding area about 50 or 60 yards ahead. My observer crossed back over to my side of the track, and we went to check it out. It was the head, neatly severed at the neck, and oddly enough, he was still wearing his glasses. He had just had a haircut. There was little or no blood; it must have bled out.

I marked the area where the head was, and then lifted it on to my towel. As it was a hand towel, it did not allow me to wrap the head but only to cover it and have the loose end of the towel draped over the face. Heads usually weigh about 10 to 12 pounds, so it was easy to carry under my arm, which I did. My observer was a bit queasy and could not bring himself to look at it or touch it, so he walked on the opposite side away from the head.

Coming towards us were the paramedic and his helper, a young coloured lad who was learning the job. As we got close enough to talk, the driver said, 'You found it then.'

With that, I lifted the corner of the towel to expose the face, and using the head like a ventriloquist dummy, I said, 'I was not lost, just asleep.' By this time, my partner was gagging, and I swear I could see the young medic turning white around his face. The senior medic and I just laughed while the other two were throwing up.

We arranged to have the body taken to the morgue at London Road Chelmsford and Essex Hospital, and I went to the morgue to see the body arrive. This was required for continuity. The officer who located the body at the scene must be at the hospital to identify that the body being brought in was the same corpse we lifted from the railway line. I found the attendant in the morgue and signed the body over to him; in turn, he signed my pocketbook with the time and date and assumed responsibility for the corpse in two parts.

The body was stripped of all clothing, which was bagged and tagged in case forensics needed to check it. We left the morgue and returned to our patrol. Two days later, I was summoned back to the morgue to explain why I had put the corpse into the fridge on a trolley feet first and placed the head on the trolley facing the door. It was so that whoever opened the fridge would be greeted with a head looking at them. Apparently, a young student nurse had opened the fridge and was so shocked that she pulled the trolley so hard it flew out of the fridge and fell on the floor. The body went one way, the head went another, and the nurse went another.

I produced my pocketbook and showed the time and date it was signed and the body handed to the attendant. That ended the enquiry for me, and we returned to patrol. The attendant who had signed my book was interviewed and said he placed the body in the fridge. The driver's wife of the other area car was a senior nurse at the hospital, so we were well informed on hospital procedures.

On the fourth of July, I left Chelmsford Police Station and joined the Force Support Unit, which was now located at HQ in Springfield, Chelmsford.

I was on duty at Southend Essex; I was driving a Force Support Unit transit and carrying a team of ten men. We were patrolling the seafront promenade, and we could see both ways along the seafront. The usual banter was going on in the van.

I could see to my right a surge in the crowd outside a pub and thought it was a fight breaking out. As I watched, I saw a man in a white suit. He was entertaining the crowd as they came towards me. My door was open, and I stood on the step to see over the crowd.

The gentleman in the white suit was an actor playing at the West Cliff Theatre. He looked like Colonel Saunders from KFC. He had white hair with a white tash and goatee beard and was wearing a white Stetson cowboy hat, which he kept taking off and sweeping it in front of him while he was taking a bow to the audience (the crowd).

My crew left the van and stood at the edge of the passing throngs. It was a nice day, and people were enjoying the good weather and the happy banter going on.

The actor we had named Buffalo Bill was close now. He spoke to me, and I fell into his trap because he spoke so quietly. He came towards me, smiling, and said something which I did not hear, so I leant out of the cab and smiled at him. He was obviously playing up to the crowd. He removed his hat and waved it at them, then he turned quickly and grabbed my shoulders and gave me a big kiss, to the delight of the crowd.

My own crew encouraged the crowd to come for a kiss and formed a queue. It was embarrassing for me. But it was a good, lighthearted atmosphere, so we all kept up the banter with the crowd. The day ended well without any trouble or arrests. The next day at the office, my in tray was filling up with requests for a date and pamphlets on joining gay clubs and so on; it only lasted until another incident came up.

Almost a year to the day, my team was directed to Westcliffe to assist in a murder enquiry. We reported to the senior CID boss at the scene. He informed us a man had been shot, and we could help with door-to-door enquiries. He also said forensic services had completed their work on the crime scene, but they were waiting for the victim to be moved, and we could look at the scene if we wished. We were showed into a room where I saw a man lying on his back on the bed. He had a gunshot wound to his right temple.

I recognised him as Buffalo Bill from last year. I was asked, 'Do you think it's suicide or not?' The penny dropped; this was a setup between my team and the CID.

I said, 'No, the guy is left-handed. The marks of a watch are on his right wrist. The wound is in the right temple, so this guy would have to be a contortionist to shoot himself in the right temple with his left hand whilst lying on his back.' They had a laugh at my expense.

I returned to the transit; it was full of firearms equipment albeit under lock and key, which I carried. I took three empty cartridges, the same calibre as used in the murder, then I returned to the boarding house and handed them to the youngest CID officer who was on door duty.

I gave the empty cases which I had cleaned and polished and told him, 'I had found one on the stairs, one on the landing, and one in the toilet.' Then I instructed him to bag and tag them and give them to his boss. I then left to get on with my enquiries. All reports were completed and handed in to CID. No one made any reference to the empty cartridges.

The SOCO men and the CID had been called back to recheck the stairs, landing, and bathroom, because they thought they had missed vital evidence. I saw the CID boss sometime later; we had a coffee together. He told me that he thought it might have been me that handed in the cases, but he'd used it as an excuse to jump on the detectives who were getting slipshod. My good relationship with the CID boss was intact.

To my knowledge, the case was not resolved and is ongoing.

I swear I did not kill the colonel for kissing me.

When I was an area car driver in Charlie Delta, I was sent to the scene of an RTA at the roundabout at Springfield Road, CD. As I got near the scene, radio transmitters were hectic. The traffic drivers, fire service engines, and ambulances were already there and deploying personnel.

A car had entered the roundabout from the Hatfield Peverel Road and heading for Springfield Road (there is a bridge over the roundabout). The driver had left the road at speed, mounted the pavement, and crashed into the supporting pillars of the bridge. The car was on fire and well alight to the extent the windows had turned black with soot on the inside.

I left my car and went to speak to the traffic drivers who warned me to stay back. The heat was horrendous, and the car could implode any second. I did not know how many people were in the car, but as I turned, I could see a pair of small hands in the soot at the top of the rear passenger window. They were sliding down the soot inside the window to the door level. At that point, the car imploded, blowing the windows out. The heat intensified, and firemen moved us away from the heat of the wreck.

I walked to one side and violently vomited. I remained at the scene until the fire was out and the bodies removed. There were two adults and two children. They were like statues made of charcoal, burnt beyond recognition as humans.

I became a casualty and was treated by paramedics. I was relieved of duty and taken home by my relief driver. It lasted four days before I could return to work. Jenn took time off to look after me. I spent a lot of time with my children when they were in the house. I was so grateful they were all okay.

As part of the support unit, my team were directed to assist in a murder enquiry at Billericay. A young barmaid from a pub in Pitsea had been found in the centre of a large cornfield by a farmer driving a combine harvester.

The rotary blades on the front of the machine had become jammed and stopped cutting the corn. The farmer got out of the cab to check the blades, and he found what he thought was the remains of a blowup sex doll. He tried to move the bits and realised it was a woman who had been dismembered by the machine.

The farmer had radioed his farm and asked them to call the police and to come and help him. When we arrived, the whole rotary section from the front of the machine had been dismantled from the machine. Most of the body parts had been collected up and placed on a clean plastic sheet. The CID and SOCO, the doctor, and the coroner's officer had all been, and the body was sent to the morgue. We sealed off the whole field, and a search of the area was to show a car had been parked at the side of the field near the road.

Casts of tyre marks were taken. We saw where the corn had been flattened inside the cornfield and where the corn had been trampled right into the middle of the field just further behind where the harvester was. Some clothing, shoes, and a handbag were recovered, bagged, and tagged.

Items from the bag gave the identity of the young lady, and forensic reports from the post-mortem autopsy revealed that sexual intercourse had taken place after death.

We assisted for a few days before being called for other duties. It turned out that the young barmaid was picked up after work by her seventeen-year-old boyfriend who lived in Billericay. He was arrested and charged with murder.

At the time of this enquiry, there were four other unsolved murder enquiries going on, which meant that all sixty men on the FSU were utilised in the enquiries. This was in addition to all firearms incidents coming in.

CHAPTER FOUR

I had my driving permit renewed. Some officers were astonished, some complained, some disgusted, and some amused. As for myself, I was very pleased. It was an achievement to get a driving permit within only three months of joining the force at Chelmsford. I felt elated and could smell and taste freedom. As well as a driving permit, I was also given a vehicle examiner's permit.

This was another credit-sized card issued by the CC (chief constable). It authorised me to road-test any vehicle at any time and to examine the brakes, wheels, tyres, exhaust systems, lights, horn, handbrake mechanism, wipers, windows, etc. for cracks or damage with or without the driver/owner on board.

To me it meant I could order a driver out of his vehicle and leave him and any other passengers where they were until I road-tested the vehicle and returned. If the vehicle was in a state of neglect or disrepair, I would call out the traffic commissioners and have them examine the vehicle. It also gave me a POA (power of arrest) if the driver/owner objected.

Only one other driver had an examiner's permit, so I just kept it quiet. You must also bear in mind, I am a time-served motor engineer fully qualified with an apprenticeship behind me. What this meant was, I could give expert evidence in court if need be.

Chelmsford had its own police station in the town centre. Its designated call sign was Charlie Delta, and its radio was in direct contact with HQ in Springfield, Chelmsford. The call sign for HQ was VG. Any messages were through HQ, were from VG. Chelmsford town, which also had direct contact with cars and messages, were prefixed Charlie Delta and directed to cars Charlie Alpha 1, 2, or 3.

Drivers adhered to a 10-code. I had to learn. I can only remember some, but not all.

10-1   Officer in the car CA 2 on duty and on patrol, double crewed

10-2   North side CD

10-3   Return to station CD

10-4   Message received, will comply

10-5   Out of car temporarily, dealing with an incident

10-6   Assisting other units

10-7   Off-air refreshments at CD

10-8   Switch to silent mode, only radio operator and driver can hear

10-9   Officer requires urgent assistance

10-10   Off duty at CD

The most important message was 10-9, and a location was very important. It was always blues and twos driving. I recall my tutor reminding me that if I was answering a 10-9 call, I could not help anyone if I did not get there. Also, he said, 'While I have no objection to speed, I would prefer if you would keep both hands on the wheel when we travel at over 100 mph.' He was right, of course. Two points which I often refer to in my mind.

The officers at CD could not understand how I could find my way around so quickly having only been driving a couple of weeks. I did not make them any the wiser the fact that I had just finished nearly eighteen months running a taxi and bus in and around the CD area and the fact that I had been working for the parks department as a dog handler.

There are twelve parks in CD, and I knew every road through each park. So I could travel from east to west through different parks and totally miss out the town centre if the need came up. It gave me great pleasure to use this knowledge and amaze my observer on occasions. On one such occasion, I had the inspector in the car. We were at Galleywood, and HQ called 10-9 at Roxwell Road. Galleywood is south of CD and about 5.7 miles from Roxwell, which is on the west side of town.

As I was near Oaklands Park, I turned into the park and cut through to Moulsham Street, around the hospital to Central park, through the park, and on to Waterhouse Lane, then turned left to the greenhouses of the parks department and across the playing field, heading for trees on a lower level. I lined the car up to a gap in the trees and told the passengers to hold on. We reached the end of the field, and I went down a ramp on to a lower-level field, turned left, and followed the edge of the field until I could see to my right the bottom of a street. There was a small wooden bridge allowing access to the park.

It had two upright posts one either side, so I turned right and headed for that street. The inspector had not spoken a single word since we went off-road. I passed between the posts with inches to spare, shot up the street, and turned left on Roxwell Road, joining the flow of traffic without stopping.

In minutes, we were at the scene of the 10-9. Out the car, I assisted the PC. We arrested two people when the other car plus traffic cars turned up. The prisoners were taken to CD in traffic cars and the PC to the hospital for a checkup. He was okay, just a few cuts. The inspector said, 'Patrol town centre until the other CD car is free.' I left the scene, and my attention was drawn to my back seat observer.

He had got into the back seat to allow the inspector in the front seat. He was shaking and laughing. He said he was 'bricking it' when we went off-road and half the time had no idea where we were. He also, said, 'The brakes on the inspector's side of the car weren't working.' He could feel him pushing into the seat, trying to brake with his imaginary pedals.

We both just laughed. I said, 'There is only one hour left on the shift. I am going to HQ to wash the car, and anyway, the boss will want to see me before I go off duty.' We cleaned and checked the car for damage and parked up at the cattle market so I could catch up on my paperwork.

I just got it done and was called, 'CA 1, report to the duty inspector CD ASAP.'

I replied, '10-4.' By now, I was at the station, left the car out front in lay-by, and went straight to the inspector's office. I was dying to laugh.

He had called the sergeant into his office as well. He said, 'Sit down. I want to talk to you about the incident we went to earlier. I have never had the pleasure of a mystery tour before.' He rambled on and obviously had more to say.

I interrupted, I said, 'As far as I am aware, I have not broken any rules or committed any offences or caused any problems, and as it is five minutes over my shift. I would like to go home unless you are willing to sign overtime for me.'

He replied, 'No overtime.'

I replied, 'We can go over this in detail in duty time tomorrow. These are my log book and incident log. Thank you and good night, sir.' And I left. I could hear the sergeant laughing after I closed the door.

The inspector never brought up the incident again, but the sergeant and I had a good laugh when we met, and so life at that time was okay. We were living at Meadgate Avenue, and I was looking at trying to buy our own place. Of course, it all takes time. Jenn and I wanted to stay in CD. We found a derelict farmhouse on Pump Lane called Evergreens.

Evergreens after the Extension and windows

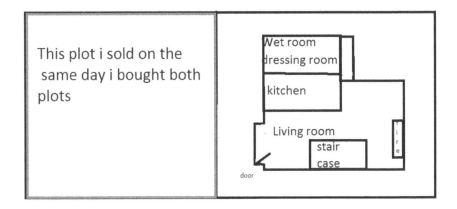

The name was branded into a piece of shaped as a tree and mounted on a piece of angle iron.

Taken over by druggies, it was stripped out inside. All wooden fixtures—i.e. doors, banisters, benches—had been used for firewood. All plumbing had been taken out and sold (scrap). All electrical fittings were missing, and every room was a basic different colour under the graffiti. But it had three bedrooms, and the kids were getting bigger. It was on the edge of a huge housing development by Fairview, the builders.

There were seven phases of this huge project. So at present, they were on to no. 3. We thought it would take at least two years before they got to us. Jenn and I liked the area and the house. We could see beyond the DIY and work needed, so we made enquiries on how we could buy it. After many heartaches and problems, I secured a 100 per cent mortgage, and the same day, we were to sign contracts.

I sold half of the plot to a builder. The boundary was marked blue and my boundary in purple.

While all this was in progress, I was still an area car driver working out of Chelmsford station. I worked on DIY and got the house ready to move in. There was a great deal of work to complete before it was finished. Jenn and I talked to the family and told them it would be untidy and not comfortable for a while with more work to be done.

They were all in favour, so Jenn organised a Friday night after our meal. It was to be a family meeting night, to discuss any problem no matter what. While at the meeting around the table, she told them to keep notes and bring them up on Friday. It did not matter what the problems were; we would discuss possible solutions and adopt them if necessary. Also, at this time, we had a sixth member, the family pet ZAK.

He lived outside in a big kennel. But he was allowed indoors only at ground level. He was a three-year-old GSD dog. Not a police dog, just a pet. This was 1974–1975. I organised builders and tradesmen to work on the house. We built an extension of fifteen by twelve on to the kitchen, which included a wet room shower, toilet, and dressing room.

We removed three internal walls and made a staircase to fit in behind were the front door used to be. We put bay windows to the front and side and made a new entrance through the old fireplace and where the chimney was. It took over one year, and we could not see an end to it.

At the same time, I had found out the force had another unit working out of a substation at Melbourne.

I made enquiries and found it was called the Force Support Unit. It was self-contained, and the personnel had to have twelve years' experience. They dealt with crowd control at football matches and really anywhere where large numbers of people gathered. They also assisted other forces when requested. I talked to some of the men and asked what it was all about and if I could apply. My probationary time was over.

So I asked for an interview with the unit boss. I got an interview and talked a long time with this man. He said there was a vacancy, and my background experience was very good. The only snag was, my shift sergeant at CD would not let me go. The boss said, 'Sit down and write an application to join FSU and have two copies printed.' He kept one copy and instructed me to go to work as normal, and he would let me know when to submit my request.

After a memo came, I submitted my copy and waited. Two days later, my shift inspector called me into his office. He talked about the unit and said he knew I had applied. He said, 'I won't stand in your way. Permission granted to go.' He then said, 'Take Saturday and Sunday off and report to Melbourne on 4 July 1976 at nine.' I was really pleased; no problems had arisen with the sergeant. So when I told Jenn, she was so pleased for me.

On Friday at the family meeting, I told the kids about my new job and said as I did not know about the shifts and times, I would need them to help me and Jenn and give them more responsibility, to take care of themselves and each other. I rang my mum and told her, and she arranged to come and visit for a week. She could get the National Express coach from Newcastle to Victoria, then Victoria to Chelmsford.

My mum brought with her copies of the local newspapers for me. She said, 'You are not going to like what you read in the *Gateshead Post*.' The centre pages was a double-page spread with passport-sized pictures of thirty police officers upwards in a rogues' gallery. They had all been arrested and charged with all kinds of offences going back years. Some went to prison; some were fined.

All were discharged from the force. They had all been involved with robberies, burglaries, and handling stolen property. They were using police vehicles to move stolen property and were using police garages to store the loot until it was moved on. These were men I had worked with for years; I even trusted them to come into my home during the night to feed the twins when they were small if I could not get home while on night shift. They even burgled my aunties home three years running. She was a rep for Avon goods. They took all her Xmas orders each year. The news really got to me.

I could not understand why I had not worked it out for myself; there were clues all over. It explained why the other dog handler always had no further action. When he committed all the offences he did, he was part of this group. He could stop them any time. I still can't believe even today. I did not realise what was going on. I would not hesitate to arrest any of them had I suspected them.

Elsdon's dog also savaged a nurse. He was posted to the far end of the county. The dog was destroyed, and the nurse took an out-of-court settlement in thousands of pounds. The whole sorry business just made me reinforce what a good decision it was for me to leave the force when I did.

Maybe as you read on, you will notice how sceptical I became. I trusted no one I came into contact with, in or out of uniform. I saw senior officers in an entirely different way to my new colleagues. The corruption and mistrust are still with me after all this time. Had it not been for Jenn, I might have gone mad. She was a very good counsellor and got me through every incident I became involved in.

She was the voice of reason, my mentor, my nurse, my best friend, my lovely wife. I am even more besotted with her now than when I was a schoolboy. She had given me three great children, and she saw to all our needs and wants. My mum enjoyed her break with us, and she got on very well with Jenn all the time. I am so lucky to have them at this time.

While still at CD, I was assigned to attend a Gymkhana along with a dozen other officers. It was a yearly event; everyone enjoyed.

The sergeant allocated everyone with jobs to supervise the event. He said, 'You're with me. Let's have a look around and see where things are.' We did look at all the stalls and sideshows, but I had the measure of the sergeant. He was a drinker and was heading for the beer tent. We ended up having a few beers more than what was good for me. I felt groggy and had to get some fresh air. I walked through the crowds who gave me some weird looks. I felt so sick I went into the woods.

I walked a while and came across a clearing with nice, well-cut grass and a hedge to break the wind. I sat down behind the hedge and relaxed. I took my helmet off and found three huge chunks of cheese in it. No wonder people were giving me weird looks. I ate some cheese and sat back leaning into the hedge.

I still felt sick but must have dozed off to sleep. I slipped over from my sitting position to lying on my right side at the bottom of the hedge. I woke up about an hour later and still felt I wanted to throw up. I must have dropped off again. I was disturbed by a terrible noise and a pounding in my head. In this half-awake state, the noise was getting nearer and louder.

I had no idea what it was until I heard, saw, and felt a lot of horses crashing through the hedge and over me. I grabbed my helmet and crawled to the edge of the hedge, then I realised I was on the damn race course under a jump. I pulled myself together and headed back through the woods.

The day had ended an hour ago, and my team, with the sergeant, had been searching for me. They asked where I had been, and I babbled some excuse about returning two lost children to their parents. It was always best to have some excuse ready. As we travelled back to CD, a message from HQ came over the radio and said, 'PC Waugh is to report to a superintendent at HQ.' The team dropped me off, and I went to the washroom and stripped to the waist and showered my head and shoulders. I dried off and checked my uniform after brushing it thoroughly.

I was now stone-cold sober and ready. I went to see the superintendent who was from the FSU I had applied to join. He was with two other senior officers who interviewed me and welcomed me to join the unit. I left and returned to CD, signed off duty, and went home. Jenn said, 'You have been drinking. Look at the state of you.'

I explained what had taken place. She said, 'You might have blown your chances turning up for an interview like that. How much have you had? And that damn sergeant should have left you out of it.' She eventually got the whole story, and we had a good laugh about it. The next day was a normal day; no one said anything.

In the next few days, I got a message to report to HQ, the Force Support Unit which had been relocated to HQ from Melbourne. I promised Jenn I would never drink alcohol, wine, or spirits ever again, and I have remained teetotal to this day.

The house was nearly done—all new fixtures to the kitchen, wet room, bedrooms. It really was coming together now, and my new position was great. Jenn and the kids worked hard and helped me all the time. I had also changed my car. I had a 365 Consul. On my first day, I was walking to HQ when a car pulled alongside me. It was another officer named Frank.

He was going to HQ FSU's new office. The unit had moved from Melbourne. He had been with the unit as a PC, passed his exams, and was coming back as a sergeant to lead a team of ten men. Once I was booked in and joined others in the parade room, the bosses came in and introduced themselves and wished me well.

They also said there was a job for us at 1300. 'Be ready to go.' I tried asking everyone what was the job and got the same answer from everyone. All jobs were on a need-to-know. 'You will be told en route.' The nearer it got to 1300, the more men were turning up. Eventually, there was a briefing. The job was at a farm in Tiptree.

We would be briefed on site, and they told me I was part of *A* shift under a new sergeant, Frank. We left HQ in convoy and headed for

Tiptree. Five other transits and two unmarked cars = sixty men. We all pulled into a car park at a farm. Everyone debussed, and we all went into a covered shed.

We were given little baskets, two each, and led out of the shed to an area at the back. I still hadn't been told anything. But what I saw was everyone picking strawberries and filling punnets. This was such a letdown, and I wondered what I had let myself in for. Frank assured me this was a one-off and that they don't come round very often.

I could really see the funny side of this diversion. I imagined we would be clearing a gyppo camp with the amount of personnel we had. Different sergeants took their teams to some ongoing jobs, and we returned to HQ. Frank told me to go with another driver and learn where to fill up and top up oils and be introduced to some of the mechanics at HQ who maintained the fleet, and so my day passed quietly. We were all learning together.

When I got home, Jenn came in with the kids. She was keen to hear if my day was exciting or not. I told her about the big buildup to the 1300 job, and when we got there, it was strawberry picking. So we all had some for tea and had a laugh about my disappointing secret job.

It did not take me long to settle in to every aspect of my new roll. There were no designated drivers, but Frank asked me to make sure I was in early and pick up the transit keys. And so I became the regular driver. Everyone just accepted this. I enjoyed being a driver again. Lots of new equipment was introduced as we were the 'heavy mob', the twenty-four-hour army. So we had to train with new gear and had our blood group painted on our riot helmet. We carried full-sized shields on the vans, gas masks, and much more. Frank was a fitness fanatic, so he had us all training in the gym, and once a month, we had to qualify with a one-mile run in full riot gear.

It was not about speed; it was about teamwork. Start together, help each other, and finish together. It also made sure you had confidence in the team when work came. Other forces were sending men to train with us, so they could teach their own forces when they returned. We were given the responsibility of controlling the football grounds at home matches in Colchester and Southend.

At this time, riots were breaking out up and down the country. Other forces requested our help when their manpower was depleted by injuries. So we travelled to places like Greater Manchester, Leicester, Liverpool, Birmingham, Nottingham, Blackpool, Leeds, Hull, Sheffield, Peterborough, Brighton, Hastings, Dover, Felixstowe, Cambridge, and many more. I was spending more and more time away from home.

As was my house name plaque Evergreens, my colleagues on the unit would take it without my knowledge wherever we went and put it in places I would find it. It had been recovered from all the above cities and many more. It continued to travel for seven years; I have emails and pictures from all over the country showing its location.

When we could, Jenn and I talked about it, and she said she was happy because we had a family, which was what she wanted, and I could chase my career. The kids had grown up now, and Jenn took a job with BT (British Telecom) to keep her busy. She also asked if I wanted any more kids and if I would consider a vasectomy if not. I said no to more kids and yes to a chop (vasectomy).

I arranged an appointment. It was for nine, and I was booked in for riot training at one. I turned up at nine and was shown into a local surgery theatre upstairs in my doctor's. I was prepared for surgery by the nurse and was on the table in the middle of the room in just a gown. The doctor came in, and the gown was rolled up to my chest. I had to lie flat on my back with my arms folded across my chest, so I could not see what was going on.

I was given an injection which numbed the whole area. The doctor was on my left, and he was facing the front of the building. He talked me through what he was doing and kept asking me if I was okay. He, more or less, had completed the work and assured me all went well. But I could not hear him because of an enormous row and noise coming from outside.

There was shouting and yelling. When I turned my head to look out of the front window, which was plain glass because we were upstairs, I saw that the traffic had come to a standstill on the main road. A double-decker bus was outside the windows; it was full of school kids who were writing scores out of 10 on their books and holding them up whilst banging on the side of the bus and screaming out of the windows.

The doctor apologised for the kids, and I said, 'It's okay. I would have to put up a score if I had been on the bus.' The nurse was giggling and said at least I had a decent score. I left the surgery and went home. The kids were at school. Jenn was at work, so I rang her and told her what had gone on. She just laughed.

I got dressed ready for training and went to work. I met up with Frank, and the team were preparing for a mile run. I told Frank what had been done; he wanted me to go home and rest. I said, 'I would kit up. I will run with the team, but I will sidestep. And if I have problems, I will drop out.' We all set off together, and it was a nice, slow pace, so I was able to sidestep all the way.

We all ended up in the shower after the run. Frank said, 'Any problems, stay at home and ring me. Take time off.' I went home, and eventually, Jenn came home. When I told her I had been training, she got mad at me and said, 'You realise most people have two or three days off after a vasectomy.' I assured her I was okay, and I was. The whole area was numb. Eventually, we went to bed.

I was sitting on the bed when Jenn came in. She was laughing and said, 'Let's have a look then.' And she jumped on to the bed. When she landed, I took off upwards. Only it felt like my genitalia weighed a ton, and it had gone black. When she saw how much pain I was in, she stopped jumping up and down, but she just shoved me on to my back and roared with laughter. We eventually dropped off to sleep.

I went to work the next day, and no one except Frank knew. Life went on. Part 2 orders were on the noticeboard and were asking for officers who had any firearms experience to apply for training. I put my name forward and was selected because of my army training with weapons. That meant training with other members of the tactical firearms group, so I learned as much as I could.

The whole firearms unit were taken from the Force Support Unit, so I knew a lot of the members. I was tested and passed the tests, so I was given a firearms permit. This permit allowed me to go to any police station in the country and show them my warrant card and my firearms permit. The station chief would then be obliged to provide any and all weapons that were named on the permit. By the time I became an instructor, after seven years, I had qualified to have twenty-seven different weapons and gases.

I graduated from a Smith & Wesson six-shot double-action revolver to shotguns and much more. Training had to be fitted in between all other things, so I became very busy. Each permit holder was tested every month, and failure to qualify meant extra training and no callouts until you regained your permit. There were no regular shifts as such. When we were called out, it was to stay until the job was completed.

It became a joke. If I came home on the same day as I went out, it was a bonus. In 1980, I was called out and told to bring an overnight bag. When I got to HQ, there were eleven officers and two inspectors already there. I was told to go and get some more clothing and my passport. This was at 6 p.m. on a Friday. There were rumours we were going to Ireland.

We were transported to London and housed in government buildings overnight; we were assembled in a huge building and were to be briefed by a government minister, Mr W. Whitelaw. There were over 400 men present. After the briefing, we were taken to Heathrow and boarded a jumbo jet bound for Africa.

We arrived at Nairobi late Sunday and transferred to another flight to Zimbabwe via Joburg and then by bombproof truck to Harare and out into the bush to set up a camp and a polling station for the election of Robert Mugabe. We spent four days in the bush protected by armed forces.

The rest of the time was spent in the township areas. The polling station was roofless; we made a makeshift roof out of tarpaulin sheets and found overnight that a swarm of killer bees had taken up residence in the sheets. We had to burn them out before polling could take place. Large queues had arrived overnight to vote. The paramilitary officers arrested one of Mugabe's henchmen for intimidation of voters waiting in the queue. He was taken to a township compound by helicopter. When we broke camp and returned to the township, I went to the compound and asked about the prisoner who had been brought in. No one knew anything about him. One of the para officers said he would have been flown over Mugabe's territory at 500 feet and thrown out as a warning to others; this was the normal practice.

We mixed with white farmers and were made welcome. The powers that be had issued the wrong malaria tablets and the wrong salt tablets, so most of the Essex contingent were ill. As we waited in the lounge at the airport for the trip home, the two inspectors fell out and ended up in fisticuffs in the main concourse, fighting like a couple of schoolkids. It was quickly stopped, and they were kept apart all the way home.

Eleven out of the twelve men went to hospital and were tested and treated for malaria and other tropical diseases. Africa is a beautiful country, but the inhabitants' lifestyles leave a lot to be desired. All females I met who were above school-leaving age carried .45-calibre handguns in their bags all the time.

Big shops had armed guards on every entrance. Areas in the townships still had no-go areas for whites. On one shopping trip, a colleague and I left a big shop via the wrong door and had only gone a few yards before we were surrounded by black locals. Fortunately, the shop doorman saw us and came to get us; he was heavily armed. The locals dispersed quickly. We were taken back into the shop, and we were allowed to leave via the front door. All was well.

On our last day, we were packing our bags to leave, and a young local lad who worked where we were staying was helping us. As a thank you, I gave him a couple of my blue uniform shirts still in the wrapping from the stores for all his help. He had the biggest smile ever, ear to ear, like he had won the lottery. We left about an hour later and were heading for the pickup point when I saw the young local lad being escorted by the paramiltary police. He was taken into an office in the next building.

I went in and enquired about him and was told he had been arrested for stealing two shirts. I asked to speak to a senior officer or whomever was in charge, and I was shown into an office where a senior officer asked if he could help me. I explained about leaving today and giving the shirts to the local boy as a gift. He picked up the phone and spoke to someone, and minutes later, an officer entered the room and showed me two shirts. The senior man asked if I could identify them for him. Fortunately, as we were leaving, I was wearing one myself. I pointed out they were uniform shirts, and if he would check, he would see the spare shirts were the same size as mine, eighteen-inch neck.

He had the young man brought in; he returned the shirts to him and released him. We left the building together then went our separate ways. It was a big lesson for me and for the young lad. Eventually, we flew home. There were over 400 on the plane, and they drank the plane dry of everything before we landed at Heathrow.

I was the only one out of twelve who did not go to the hospital. I took three days off and enjoyed Jenn's company and told her about the trip and how much I missed her and how much I loved her. I was so pleased to be back with her. Jenn commented, 'That was some call-out.' In London, every man had been given some expenses. As I had saved mine, I gave it to Jenn as a present, £200, and we enjoyed a spending spree.

This was the same year the girls decided they did not want to come on a holiday with Jenn and me and were going to Spain with their friends. Jenn and I both shouted, 'Yippee! We are free. Go to Spain and have a lovely time.' As they were eighteen now, Jenn and I had a long good talk with them about travel and airports, conduct, foreign police forces not being like the UK, zero tolerance towards youngsters abroad, drunkenness, lewdness in public places, etc. We had every faith in the girls, and they did not let us down.

So Jenn and I decided to have a holiday as well. We booked a hotel in Gozo, an island in the Mediterranean in the Maltese group. Little did we know what effect this would have in our future. In the next few years, we had two to three breaks from work, and we tried Ibiza, Benidorm, the Maldives, Balearic Islands, the Canaries, the Channel Islands. We kept returning to Gozo. The people were friendly, and we soon got the hang of lira and cents.

Jenn and I travelled extensively across Europe and spent a lot of time in France, Belgium, Germany, Switzerland, Italy, Sicily, Cyprus and the islands, the Netherlands, and more, so much so we got fed up with flying and airports. So we decided we would go by road and ferries. We also decided we would return to Gozo and make it a base for ourselves.

I became the English agent for the Serena Hotel ran by Joe and Maryrose Vella and family. I sent a lot of people over, and a lot still remained good friends. Jenn and I liked Gozo so much we talked about retiring out there. At this time, I still had fifteen years to go before I could retire and eight years to go to get my time in the force to thirty years.

Nevertheless, we talked about it and dreamt about it. we decided to look for a place to buy, and we found a villa in Gharb, one of a group of three. It was out of town and not in a tourist area. The building was in the early stages. Jenn said it would be great to have somewhere we could all share. See pictures of the early stages.

So we went ahead and bought the land and engaged the builders to build in stages. We were the first English people to secure a penalty clause on the contract with the builders' mind. We were not going in blind; we engaged an advocate to oversee all work and contracts we needed. His name is Michael Grech. He also became a silent partner in a private co I set up because I intended to buy a boat and take friends out on it. This was all in preparation for the distant future. Michael was our link to the Maltese government, and he made sure everything was in order when we were not on the island.

We became very friendly and got to know his family. At this time, I also owned a twenty-five-foot powerboat, Derek, and I took it out on weekends and days off. I had also upgraded my car to a four-and-a-half-litre Range Rover, so no problems towing the boat, except the trailer was useless and dangerous. I located a company that specialised in making trailers made to measure. I engaged this company to build me a trailer. The guy in charge made a trailer to match the rover's same wheelbase, and the wheels were spaced out, to make for ease in handling the rig. One person could launch or recover the boat without help. The centre of gravity was very low in the centre of the boat and trailer.

The overall length of the whole rig was forty-five feet, and altogether fully loaded, it weighed approximately five tons. So now we decided to take the boat to Gozo overland. Jenn wanted to learn how and familiarised herself with driving and reversing the rig.

We practised reversing all around an industrial estate. Eventually, she was satisfied the rig was not a problem. So we decided to give it a test run to Kent to visit her sister. Jenn drove it on the way, and she tried at various speeds—thirty, forty, fifty miles per hour. It stayed in line with breaking hard, perfect. I tested it on the return journey and deliberately took the speed up higher than the limit (no cameras those days). It broke always in a straight line and showed no signs of swaying at all.

So we sat at home and worked out the best time to make the trip as it was January. We set a time in August. I could take my summer leave up to the end of August for two weeks, and I could link that to my winter leave two weeks in September. I could also apply for days off in lieu of overtime owed to me.

So throughout the year, I filled in application forms for single days and double days off in September and got different bosses to sign and approve the time off. The end result was, I was covered for six weeks and two days off consecutively. No one worked it out, so it was official. We planned to leave on 25 August, Saturday.

The girls had had enough of Spain and holidays on their own. So we booked them in at the Serena from Monday, 27 August. They would fly out, and Jenn and I would get there hopefully in their first week. Derek, at this time, was living away from home, so he didn't manage to make this holiday. We prepared for nearly a year. Insurance was covered by AA five-star cover for ourselves and the rig.

We also got the AA to plan an overland route, avoiding the mountains. They sent us maps and recommended routes which would take us through France, Belgium, Switzerland, and Italy, via the western highway through Italy, and ferry from Palermo, Sicily, to Malta via Tunisia. I had extra lights fitted on the trailer and the rover and extra mirrors on the wings. It looked massive.

All the paperwork was in order—passports, insurance, etc. At last we were nearly ready. Work went on as usual for me, trying to fit everything in and getting it right. I had been to Hatfield Peverel and was returning home about three and was driving along the A12 towards Chelmsford. I approached the slip road to come off the A12 at Springfield.

I was decreasing speed in readiness for the turn off at about fifty miles per hour. Traffic was light. Just before the turn-off, I heard the rear passenger door click shut. I also felt a change in the car temperature. I looked in my rearview mirror and saw a young lady sitting in the middle of the rear seat. She looked like a teenager with long blonde ponytail.

Our eyes met in the mirror, and she said, 'Don't worry. I will be leaving soon. You are going past my home.' By now I had come down the slip road, around the roundabout, and turned into Pump Lane. She said, 'I often see you. You live in the cottages. So do I. Only I live in the second cottage. Thank you for the lift.'

Again I felt a change in temperature and heard the door click. She was gone. I just went home and told Jenn. At first she just took the mickey, but I convinced her it had happened. Neither of us had any explanation.

Over a week later, I had a session of training at an outdoor range near Braintree. This was privately owned, and the farmer used to come and join in training and generally helping. During a break, I was telling some of the guys about my mysterious passenger.

They laughed, and the mickey taking started. Then the farmer who had heard my story spoke up. He said, 'Did the girl get out at the first pair of cottages on the right?'

I replied, 'Yes.'

He said, 'My grandfather owned those cottages and the farm. He lived in the second cottage, and his daughter was killed on the A12 where you described. She was on a motorbike. I have pictures at home. She was eighteen at the time. I will pop home and get a photo and bring it back.' Which he did, and the photo was the girl whom I saw in the mirror. No one knew what to say after we looked at the picture. I just kept an open mind and accepted what happened really did take place. The accident happened fifty years previously, when she was killed circa 1925, before I was born.

Jenn and I both managed to get away for a couple of weeks, and we booked a holiday in Agadir, Morocco. It was a disaster from the outset. We chose a hotel and, upon arrival, were shown two adjoining ground floor rooms. They were filthy and full of cats (approximately twenty to twenty-five). We refused to accept this, and after a huge row in the hotel, we took an alternative flat three stories up. Access was an external staircase, which seemed to go on forever.

We struggled with our cases up these steep stairs, and on the outside wall, which also went up like the stairs, cats were sitting on the ledges in the sun. Jenn was ahead of me, and I vented my temper on the cats by pushing them off the wall with my elbow on each step I took. We eventually got into the flat and unpacked a few things. Eventually, we ventured out to look for a cafe.

There were several choices, but we passed by them. They all looked scruffy. We kept looking and eventually found a place which had tablecloths and glasses on the tables. We entered and were shown to a table. We ordered food, and whilst we waited, we had time to look around. The tables were in a large yard which was covered by a trellis work structure with greenery growing like a vine. It shaded us from the sun and was very nice.

Except I could see holes through the greenery. When we had been served and had eaten, Jenn asked the waiter why there were holes in the greenery. He explained that about two hours earlier, they had to close the cafe and get everyone out because there were cats crashing through the greenery and landing on the customers and tables. He said it was raining cats.

Jenn and I thanked him for the meal, and we left. When we got our bearings, we had walked all the way around the block and were back at our flat, which overlooked the cafe. I never mentioned about elbowing the cats off the staircase wall to Jenn, but she knew.

My punishment was, I got the deli belly, sickness and diarrhoea. I was ill for three days before I could venture out. Jenn decided we should go to the embassy and see if we could go home early. We were told we would have to wait until Monday before it would be open.

So it was another couple of days in bed. We asked directions to the embassy and were told we should go through the market, and on that main road, we could get a taxi, which I thought was strange. But I never found out why no taxis came to the hotel. Monday came, and I was a little better, well enough to go to the embassy.

Jenn and I entered the vast market with dozens of little shops there. The crowds of people were dense. I had to take Jenn's hand and push my way through. I was confronted by a man with a mutilated arm; he pushed the stump of his arm in my face and shouted for money.

I just brushed him to one side and kept going when the guy was there again, waving his arm in my face and shouting for money. There were so many goods, mainly carpets all hanging from the ceiling. You had to stoop under them. I managed to get past the beggar and got Jenn ahead of me. We could see we were nearly out of there.

When I felt a hefty punch in the back, my instincts and training made me bend forward and turn, and it was the beggar still screaming at me for money. As I stood up, I hit this guy under the ribcage and sent him flying up into all the carpets, which began to fall, and Jenn and I ran clear and jumped into a taxi. It seemed the whole place collapsed, and all the shopkeepers were running after us cursing.

There must have been about 100 people running towards the taxi. The driver saw this, and he took off like a Formula One driver. Even he was screaming at us. We escaped and got to the embassy only to be told there were no early flights leaving. We were stuck there for another week. After a couple of days, I felt a bit better and ventured out. We ordered a meal at a different cafe and sat outside to eat it with other holidaymakers.

Halfway through the meal, an Arab with a monkey came to the table. He wanted the monkey to do tricks for money. It was on a lead like a dog. He moved our plates and made room for the monkey to sit on the table. It helped itself to food off my plate. That was just about enough. Jenn shoved her chair away from the table. The Arab pulled a stick out of his robe, like a chair leg, which he placed under the monkey's chin, then he whacked it, and it jumped in a backwards somersault off the table. It must have been its routine because the monkey got back on the table and clapped its hands. Jenn and I just left. We did not want another riot. We eventually got to the airport to fly home. The plane took off, and I spent the whole flight in the toilet. Jenn told me everyone on the plane was complaining about the awful smell I was causing. We arrived back in the UK, and I went straight to the chemist for help. He gave me tablets, and my sickness eased up. Jenn drove us home. What a couple of weeks, worst holiday ever.

On a separate occasion, we were traveling by road through Italy. The weather was awful—very heavy rain. Cars were being swept off the roads by water coming from the hills and down the side streets and forming fast-flowing streams across us. We got off the road for a while, but the rain did not ease up. We decided to join the toll roads on the motorways to give us a chance to get out of the low-lying valleys.

We went a little further and turned left to pick up the toll road. The storm got worse, and we got higher. It became very foggy; visibility was down to a few feet. The sun roof on the car was leaking even though I opened it and put a towel in to seal it better. It still let so much water into the car. Jenn and I were soaking wet. I kept going uphill for ages, and it got worse. The fog was so bad I could not see much.

We passed a house on my left, and I saw a place to park alongside. I was forced to stop because of the fog. So Jenn and I just waited, and we had spare shirts, so at least we could put on something dry. After about one hour, the rain stopped, and typically the sun came out. Lovely! And the fog lifted.

We got out of the car and realised it was not fog we were in. We were so high up we were in the clouds. We walked around the car, and about six feet from the side and front was a sheer drop into the valley. The occupants of the house told us it was nearly a kilometre to the bottom. They gave us tea and guided us on to the toll road, where we continued our journey.

We had no timetable and were not worried how long it would take; we just picked a hotel, stayed overnight, and had a good bath and meals and change of clothing. We decided to get south as quickly as possible.

So after breakfast, we continued through Northern Italy and chose the western highway through Genoa and on to the south to Livorno, Rome, Napoli (Naples), Cosenza, and Reggio di Calabria, where we would stay overnight and catch a ferry to Sicily. We stopped for meals and toilets but kept moving. It was eight hours behind the wheel for over 800 miles. Of course, in those days, there were no cameras or limits like there are today.

As we boarded the ferry, we chatted to lorry drivers. Apparently, they were enjoying our trip. My car had English plates which they saw in Livorno. After that, the drivers were guessing which route I would take. They were in contact on CB radio and made a game of it—who could spot me and where—and reported it to the others. None of them believed I was the driver the whole journey. We all boarded the ferry and went to Tunisia and on to Malta.

We did this trip over four separate times because we were fed up of flying. We also varied the routes as much as we could—France, Belgium, Germany, Switzerland, etc. It was a great time for us. On one trip, we went through the Mont Blanc Tunnel from France to Italy. Jenn was driving, the Range Rover towing a three-ton boat and trailer.

As she entered the tunnel, we waited to get between two heavy vehicles so they would guide us through sixteen kilometres of dark tunnel. Jenn had just got settled at about seventy to seventy-five miles per hour with the lorries when a shower of sparks showered her legs from under the dashboard. I ended up lying on my back, head on Jenn's knees, and sorted out the shorts on the wiring loom.

Jenn kept her cool and continued all the way through. I made a temporary repair, and we eventually flew out of the tunnel and pulled into a picnic area. Jenn parked the rig, opened the door, jumped out on to a grassy area, and lay flat on her back, arms and legs spread. And she released a yell to wake the dead. We had an audience of picnickers all coming to help and shouting in different languages.

It was hilarious. We continued on and eventually arrived in Gozo. The rules for the importing of vehicles were, you could only keep your car on the island for one year. Then it had to leave. We got round this by taking a ferry to Sicily and back. Our passport stamped with a new date, so we were okay for another year. We also bought a new car in the UK and came to collect it. We gave my old car to family.

It was customary to play pranks on all who worked with you, and many times, I bore the brunt of jokes, especially with my Geordie accent. They would try to put you in a position of embarrassment or to scare you. I also took part and played pranks on others at work. In Chelmsford, there was a four-story building situated as the last building before the bridge in the High Street CD opposite the old picture house. It was possible to drive on to the roof from the rear of the property.

From this vantage point, we could see most of the High Street and surrounding areas. So when it was quiet (during night shift or early hours of the morning), I would drive up and watch the High Street for a while, especially if there was a rookie on the town beat. Also, on the roof were waste bins, and one from the electric supply shop usually had light bulbs in it. On more than one occasion, the rookie would be working his way down the High Street, trying shop doors and making sure they were all secure.

We would select a couple of old bulbs—the bigger the better— and wait for the rookie, and as he passed below, we would drop the bulbs. When they hit the ground, they would explode like bombs just behind the rookie. Some would stop and run into the recess of the doorway. Some would just run like the wind over the bridge and out of sight. The fun was shared once the rookie radioed the station to tell the sergeant and ask what to do. Every radio was live, and all personnel could hear and chip in. When the shift were in for a break, the tormenting and mickey taking would start. One of the beat men was so sure he would not be caught out that he bragged about how he would sort out whoever was responsible.

His turn on nights came around again, and we waited until four thirty. We were on the roof and ready, waiting for him to come. We had a huge empty waste bin on the edge of the roof at the front of an alley between the buildings. We waited until the beat man was crossing the entrance to the alley. The timing was perfect. When that bin hit the ground, it was horrendously deafening at four thirty-five.

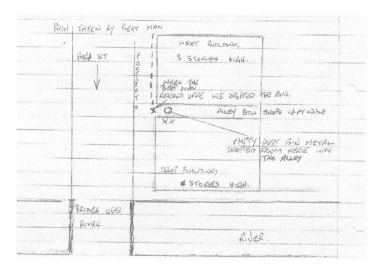

The beat man took off and disappeared down the High Street out of sight. Invariably, the memos and cartoon drawings would appear on noticeboards everywhere. The mickey taking would continue until the next event happened. Any and all the rubbish or debris caused during these pranks were meticulously cleaned up and removed before members of the public would use the areas.

One of the dog handlers had been to the abattoir for a sheep's head and meat for his dog. While he was there, the staff sneaked a pair of cow's front legs into his van. He did not notice until much later. These legs ended up in the underground car park of the police station and under the rear wheels of the boss's car. He drove over them and stopped to see what he had run over. He took one look at the cow's legs, jumped in his car, and left. No way was he going to be involved with them.

The legs ended up in various silly places and caused a lot of humour. I was on nights again, and one of the legs was still around. After our break, someone had taken the leg and put it in the post office box at the GPO main office on the corner of the High Street opposite the shire hall. We all left the station and hid in the garden at the rear of the shire hall. The beat man had been held up until everyone was in place and waiting for him to leave the station.

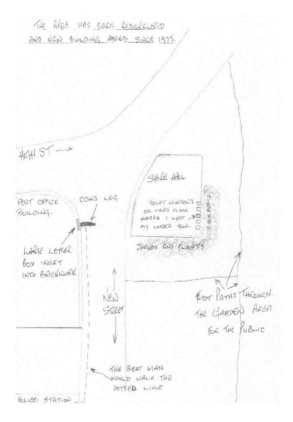

I cannot remember the exact words, but the saga went along these lines. The beat man had a silly, high-pitched voice, and the sergeant a very deep one. 'Hello, CD town beat man, over.'

The sergeant replied, 'Yeah, what do you want?'

'There is a cow's leg sticking out of the post office letterbox. What shall I do?'

'See if it has any stamps on it.'

'No stamps.'

'Has it got a postal address or label on it?'

'I'll have a look. No labels or tags.'

'Have you looked inside the box? Is the rest of the cow in there?'

'My torch has gone out. I can't see inside, Sarge.'

'Put your hand in. See if you can feel anything, and be careful, it may bite you.'

'Ow, ow, ow, something sharp stuck in the back of my hand. It's got blood on it.'

'Why have you not got your gloves on?'

'I took them off to fix my torch. It's working now. There is no cow in there, just steel spikes.'

'Yes, they are to stop people stealing from the box and to stop cows getting out.'

'What shall I do now, Sarge?'

'Get yourself back here, and I'll give you a sticking plaster and a cuddle.'

'Okay, Sarge.'

I am now going to go forward in time to fit in an interesting firearms job. This was a siege which started in Melbourne and ended in Harwich, twenty-seven hours later. I was paired up with another officer, Tab Hunter. We were sent to an address in Melbourne, to watch and wait. A burglary had taken place at a farm, and the felon had taken some firearms—two air riffles and a shotgun—and other ammunition and a backpack.

He was suspected of being on his way to his girlfriend's house, where Bob (Tab) and I were waiting. It was early afternoon, so it was daylight and was bright. We waited and waited, parked up in an unmarked car, but as we were on duty at HQ, we were in uniform.

We were in a short cul-de-sac with the end blocked off by fencing. The only way for the felon was to come from behind us. We managed to get between other parked cars, which gave us some cover. It was a short cul-de-sac, so all the cars were facing the fence across the dead end. We were also monitoring the radios for any updates.

I was in the driver's seat, and I saw the target coming towards us in the rearview mirror. I alerted Tab, and we sank down in our seats! Too late, we had been spotted, and the target crossed the street and walked past us towards the fence. He must have realised he was trapped, so he checked the fence and decided to come back towards us. We shouted warnings that we were armed police and told him to stand still.

As we approached him, he turned and ran into the nearest house. Tab and I took cover behind parked vehicles and waited. A few minutes went by, and the target emerged from the house with a man in front of him. It was obvious he was holding the man hostage as he held a shotgun against his neck. We shouted more warnings, but he ignored us and made the hostage open his car and get into the driver's seat.

He got into the back and kept the shotgun pointing at the hostage's neck. Tab and I returned to our car, and we were going to try and block him in. It was too narrow, and parked cars hindered us, so he squeezed through a gap we were making smaller and drove off towards the town centre.

All we could do was to keep an open mike and give a running commentary of events as they unfolded in front of us. We could hear other police cars nearby. As we chased the target, he made the hostage drive under thirty miles per hour and safely. We were one car back from the target, and he turned into the town centre going past the Marconi Building. There was a filling station where the target pulled on to a fuel pump; the driver was made to get out and fill up the car.

Tab and I pulled in on the forecourt, but there was too much activity and members of the public about. We told the cashier to lock the door and wait until we had gone. She did this immediately. I took up a position behind a customer's car and aimed my shotgun at the target.

The hostage filled the car and got back into the driver's seat with the villain behind him. They set off towards the police station on New Street and turned left into Victoria Road, then right into Springfield Road, left into High Street, Chelmsford. Then they went out on to Parkway and towards the Arm and Navy roundabout and left on A12 towards Colchester. Tab and I were right behind the hostage car and continued with our running commentary.

A lot of other police vehicles were joining us and forming a huge convoy. At one point, a traffic car who did not recognise our unmarked car forced his way between myself and the target car. He forced us to drop back. Tab was on a personal radio to HQ, explaining what was happening, and the traffic car was ordered to abort his position and allow Tab and I to take up no. 1 position, eyeball on target, and continue with updates and directions. We bypassed Colchester on A12, picked up the A137, and turned going to Ipswich. The target must have realised his mistake, and at a roundabout in Manningtree, we doubled back to pick up the A120 to Harwich.

As we were now travelling the opposite direction to the convoy, the villain was taking pot shots at the marked cars. We picked up the A120 and went into Harwich. We went through Harwich to what used to be a navel yard with a boundary fence of strong wire mesh. It had now become a timber yard and had piles of timber some twelve to fifteen feet high. There was a cargo ship against the quayside with gangways down into the yard. The target stopped the hostage car at the gangway, and he made the hostage lead him on to the boat.

Tab and I abandoned our car and climbed up a pile of timber, so we were at the same height as the wheelhouse on the boat. We had a good view on to the boat and could see the target and hostage in the wheelhouse. Again, we relayed a commentary to HQ, who were collating all messages and directing other officers to strategic positions in order to stop the villain from leaving the yard. It was still daylight, and now it was a waiting game until more firearms officers arrived.

They arrived, and we were deployed to cover the bow (front) and stern (back) of the boat. The yard was secured by a driver parking a great, big artic lorry across the entry gate to the yard. By this time, the target and hostage left the wheelhouse on the waterside of the boat. We learned there was a skeleton crew of five working on the boat. Next, we heard gunshots but could not see anything. Seconds later, the villain and hostage reappeared in the wheelhouse.

The villain was trying to start the boat engines by pressing buttons. Machines on board were starting up, lights going on and off. After approximately ten to fifteen minutes, he gave up and began to gather a lot of clothing and piled it all beside the door, set fire to it, and made the hostage hold the door open while he pushed and kicked the burning clothing into the hold, which was full of new cars. He then decided to leave the boat by the stern gangway, forcing the hostage ahead of him. Their car was nowhere to be seen.

It had been removed by officers. But at the bottom of the gangway was a firearms transit which had been abandoned. As the villain came down the gangway, he made the hostage drive the transit, which had the keys left in it. They went into the entrance gate and saw it was blocked by a lorry. So then they toured the yard, looking for a way out. Some of the FSU commandeered our unmarked car and chased the villain. Tab and I were left at the yard.

We heard on the personal radio the villain had crashed the fence and broke out. At the same time, they crashed into a passing ambulance, causing mayhem and damage to both vehicles. They drove out of Harwich a short way before steam and smoke from under the bonnet brought the vehicle to a halt. From that position, they could see down a side road to a pub about half a mile away.

They freewheeled to the pub and dumped the transit van. The villain cleared everyone out of the pub, including the owner. The pub was surrounded on all sides by the firearms team, and they managed to get a phone to the villain to negotiate. He ignored everything going on around him.

A forward command post was set up in a house opposite the pub. The villain kept firing his shotgun at anyone he saw move. On one occasion, he shot at a police officer who was rushed to the hospital with non-life threatening injuries (he forgot to duck). The officer was behind a car, but not low enough. The top of his head was above the level of the car roof. When the villain fired, the contents of the cartridge hit the roof and the officer's head.

We now know the pub was the Castle Inn, the villain was Paul Howe, and the hostage was John Ridley, twenty-three years old. Howe, the target, fired so regularly we got used to listening for his shots. The landlord of the pub told the officers in the FCP forward command post that he had been shooting that morning and that his gun was in the cellar and not put away, together with a large number of cartridges. The shots from Howe continued for another hour.

The Castle Inn had been nominated as pub of the year, and it was decorated with dozens of Toby Jugs everywhere. The organisers of the pub competition were coming next day to make presentations. The target was moving around the pub ground floor, upstairs, and eventually downstairs to the cellar. He located the owner's sixteen-gauge shotgun and all the ammunition. The next shot fired was not just a bang but a deafening explosion. So all the containment officers were told to double-check their cover protection at their positions.

Tab and I were given the job of evacuating the houses opposite the pub. In the last house was a young family. We got them out the back, and they were going to relatives nearby. The lady said if we were hungry, we could eat their takeaway meal and just lock the door when we left. We had been on duty since 9 a.m., and it was now thirteen hours since we had eaten. We put out the light and opened the curtains.

From the streetlights and the pub lights, we had a grandstand view of what was going on. Officers were behind a car about twenty feet in front of us. They were just relaxing in turns—one watching the pub, the other one resting. I was tempted to offer them a chip but decided not to.

The siege went on for hours. It was decided to keep it as a siege and not send in a raid team yet. Tab and I locked up the house and went to the command post. We were then given the job of relieving each pair of containment officers so they could have food and toilet facilities. The target continued his firing, so everyone was on edge. Tab and I relieved the rear garden officers. While we covered their position, Howe had set a fire in the ground floor of the pub.

The hostage took the opportunity of getting out of an upstairs window and on to a flat roof. He ran across the roof and leapt off into the beer garden. He was immediately taken to the command post where he disclosed the target was planning to leave the pub at 7 a.m. and give up. The fire was raging in the pub, and the fire service officers were standing by. The target left the pub and came to the rear fence. He saw Tab and me, and he levelled his shotgun at us. Tab and I both rolled to the left twice, and the shot from the target tore into the ground where we had been. We retreated into the trees for better cover.

The target crossed the yard. As we took cover, Frank fired a warning shot, which went above the target and hit the six-foot fence at the top. A lot of the shot tore through the foliage where we were. That shot made the villain turn and walk towards the open road. Frank was shouting warnings at him that he was facing armed officers. The target checked his gun and lifted it to fire. There was a shot fired by Frank which hit the villain in the neck and upper chest. He collapsed in a heap and was arrested and cuffed by other officers.

The paramedics attended to him immediately. The fire service went into the pub and got the fire under control. The villain was taken to the hospital and declared DOA (dead on arrival). A message from forward control said all personnel to stand down and report to FCP. The whole area was attended by SOCO to gather evidence for the inquest by the coroner.

All officers were detailed other jobs to perform. Tab and I were sent to Harwich Police Station. We were to check in all firearms from personnel. All ammunition had to be recorded and logged, and weapons to be stored. The only place at Harwich was the top floor, a large open area with a portable partition dividing the space in two. Personnel from Harwich were on one side; people on the opposite of the partition were unknown to us. The villain's family, relatives, and friends had gathered. Even his priest was there, and maybe a dozen or more people. These people had been there for hours.

One of them asked from the other side of the partition. 'Is it over?'

Someone said, 'Yes, he's dead. They blew his head off.' The partition was then pushed over. All these people were shouting and screaming. There were firearms everywhere. Very soon the place was overwhelmed with officers, and some semblance of order was restored.

Frank had been taken to HQ by a senior officer for counselling.

As officers were handing weapons in, I noticed that each of them was affected in one way or another. Some were trembling and shaking. Some could not speak. One had a lump on the side of his neck, like he had swallowed an orange. Others were crying; some could not stop talking.

None of them had any idea of what the procedure was in a case like this. So I ended up answering a lot of questions. Some of the officers wanted to give me their permits. I told them to be at HQ at 10 a.m. the next day, and we would sort everything out. The next day, seventeen men handed in their firearms permits. They would not be detailed for any firearms duties in the future.

Frank was taken off firearms duty and FSU duty. He accepted a posting to Stanway traffic. He lived in Colchester, so it was a good move. The siege was a tragic loss of life for a young man. It caused a lot of trauma for all his family and friends, not to mention the seventeen firearms officers who chose to hand in their firearms permits. With the loss of seventeen members, there was a big reshuffle at the FSU (Force Support Unit) and the Tactical Firearms Unit.

I found myself moving up the pecking order because all the replacement men were younger, more keen, and more energetic. So I had to up my performance in every aspect to keep ahead of the physical side of the work. Lots of the new guys came for advice, and when I asked, 'Why me?' They all said I was easy to talk to and trusted me. This did not go unnoticed by the bosses.

I was called into the office for an assessment by the senior officers. Firstly, they apologised for not recognising I had been on the firearms unit more than three years, which was laid down as a guide maximum for all officers. I had been there seven years.

The big problem was, there was no one with my level of experience to replace me. So I suggested I could come off the front line response and join the instructors at HQ to train and teach the younger men. That meant I would work eight to four, Monday to Friday, and have weekends off. I would also remain on call for any big or serious job that came in and could go as an observer with the team rather than take an active part and could work in an advisory capacity if the team requested it.

This was an acceptable solution which the bosses agreed with. I was to start immediately and was given the rank of an acting sergeant. This meant a pay raise. So I was now a sergeant with sergeants pay without passing exams. I worked from an office in HQ and remained to live at Pump Lane. Firearms courses for instructors were rare, so I had to wait for a course to come up.

The office was run by Sergeant Chris. There were two other instructors. No. 1 in the county was Peter Woodcock; no. 2, Bill

Bishop; and no. 3, myself. We all got on well most of the time. The inspector was Monty, and the resident armourer and instructor was Gus. He worked mainly in the armoury, range, and workshop in HQ. I was in daily contact with them all. Gus turned out to be a great help. He guided and taught me many things on and about people and subjects, right across the spectrum of firearms and teaching and lecturing.

Many firearms jobs came in, which I attended. My workload increased, and I was given the responsibility of planning, selecting, training, and running a sixteen-man sniper team. I found that more personnel were turning up on my training days, men from CID and the Regional Crime Squad. I had been working with Bill and Peter for years now. I did not always agree with them.

When they asked about various methods of training which I promoted, which were different to theirs, rows and arguments broke out. I refused to teach students parrot fashion, like schoolkids learning times tables which was how Pete and Bill were doing, on the instruction of Monty. I thought it was dangerous and did not give officers time to adapt to changing ongoing situations.

I devised exercises which meant they had to think on their feet and do whatever was needed to save lives, including theirs. I also tried to make it different, so I organised a train with several carriages to be searched. I also got permission to search an aircraft at Stansted and many other activities which had cropped up previously for me, but not the students. When I refer to students, please bear in mind that these people are not young schoolkids; they are very mature and experienced officers.

A lot of the work was at Stansted Airport. All EL AL flights had to be under armed guard all the time they were on the ground. The crew who were all armed had to leave their weapons on board in a box sealed by our customs men until the plane took off again. There were incidents when EL AL crew were stopped and searched when leaving the aircraft.

In addition to this, we had several incidents when hijacked aircraft landed at Stansted. These aircraft were guided into a special parking bay were the ground had been built up on three sides, so the top of the mounds were just higher than the level of the plane's windows, which meant when snipers were deployed, they could see into the craft. Within half an hour of the craft being in this bay, all snipers could be issued with photographs of every passenger in every seat. We also had to liaise with the army, i.e. the SAS unit, who would be deployed to board the craft and arrest everyone on board until they were identified. All in all, I was very busy, really enjoying my job.

My home life was better than ever. I was able to join in the family activities as well as teach them DIY and how to use tools safely. The family were growing up fast. We still held our Friday meetings to air any grievances. They were growing more independent of Jenn and me and were having holidays abroad without us. Our villa in Gozo was coming along nicely; building work was progressing. Jenn had now gone back to work at British Telecom as an engineer's controller. We had acquired another car for Jenn; it was a Daimler Jaguar. All was well with us. Work and lecturing kept me busy. Lots of incidents were dangerous, but with good training, they were concluded without loss of life. As I mentioned earlier, we were planning a six-week holiday trip to take our boat overland to Gozo. Time was getting on, and we were all prepared. We were going on Saturday, 25 August '84. The best-laid plans do not always happen. Sod's law, bad luck, call it what you will; it happens.

On Wednesday, twenty-second, I was at work in a classroom with twenty-plus officers when I was told to go to the armoury, and Bill would take over my class. At the armoury, I was told to take weapons to dispatch a bull, which had escaped from the abattoir and had run into town and was now in someone's back garden. I selected a small carbine riffle and a shot gun, plus my personal handgun. Upon the arrival at the location, I saw many employees from the abattoir all just waiting for me. I locked the car and went to see where the bull was.

I was met by the lady of the house, which had beautiful gardens all round, and it was well maintained and newly painted. She was ever so concerned about the safety of the bull and wanted to know if I was going to tranquilise it. I said, 'Yes, I would take care of it.' I saw it in the rear garden—3/4 of a ton of terrified beast snorting and grunting. He had ran about a mile along the railway embankment and tumbled into this garden. I brought my loaded carbine rifle and went into the adjoining garden and picked a spot about twenty feet away from the bull. I took aim and fired and hit the bull a good clean shot between the eyes. The bull's legs telescoped up into his body, and he fell.

I reloaded, and the bull lifted his head right over backwards. I fired again through its neck and into its brain. It rolled over almost immediately. The abattoir men rushed in and put a coupling on its rear leg. A crane parked in the street swung its gib over the house, and it was attached to the bull's rear leg. Other workers cut its throat from ear to ear. Apparently, if the blood is not released as soon as the bull is dead, it can ruin the meat.

The crane hoisted the bull up and swung it across the garden and over the roof. I have never seen as much blood at one time. As it was being lifted, the blood poured into the fish pond, went across the lawn, and up over the roof. Blood was running down the roof tiles and down the windows and walls. The front of the house was also ruined with blood everywhere. The lady of the house ran after me to my car. She used the most foul language and expletives to me, which I can't repeat; she was really upset, irate, fuming, hysterical.

I was just glad to get away. I went to the abattoir and spoke to the foreman and asked if there was any chance of tracing the bullets. He said, 'Come back after lunch.' This caused an almighty row with Bill because he was stuck with my students. I went back to the abattoir. The foreman had the removed head. It was on the table, and he had pushed wires through the entry holes of my bullets and out the exit holes. He then got a small chainsaw and laid it on the wires; he cut the head completely in half, and it exposed the animal's brain cavity. Both bullets had passed through the brain cavity and had crossed in the middle of the cavity. We photographed it from all angles to use for training purposes, like a visual aid.

By now it was well into the afternoon. I went back to the armoury, cleaned my rifle, and stored it away. I was given a great telling off by Gus for not retrieving my empty cartridge cases. He took my good feeling away and left me wondering if I would ever get another chance to dispatch a bull. En route to the office, Bill caught up to me; he started moaning about being lumbered with my students. A great row erupted and continued into the office until I decided I had just about enough and just walked out and went home. It was 4.30 p.m. Anyway, Jenn had finished early and was at home, and she had made a lovely dinner just ready to serve as I walked in. I sat and enjoyed my dinner and Jenn's company.

She said, 'Your very quiet. What's going on? Bad day at the office?' And at that point, the phone rang. Jenn answered it and said, 'Your day is not over yet. You are wanted at HQ.' Little did I know that the incident that followed was to be life-changing for a number of people. It was a call-out to arrest an armed robber at Walton-on-the-Naze. Bill was already at HQ, and he was still in a temper. Together, we loaded the van with various weapons and personal guns for officers to be picked up en route. A young CID officer had been roped in; he was new to firearms and only trained up to containment level. I doubted his experience and ability firearms-wise. We picked up Peter, the no. 1 instructor, and stopped at Colchester to pick up another sergeant, Mervyn Fairweather.

We continued on to Walton and were met by officers who had been on duty all day. The firearms men were assembled, and Bill and Pete were to each lead a team of four, and we were to go to an area in Frinton, a few miles along the coast, where we were to wait for the appearance of the target on the plot, who would be coming to recover the money, the proceeds of two robberies carried out during the afternoon, which he had hidden in the wooded area close to where we were.

Bill and Pete went to survey the area and to select teams and came up with a plan. Pete surrounded himself with three very experienced men with long service in firearms department. I had Pete down as a coward because of past incidents. That left Bill, the Colchester sergeant, Mervyn (whom I was about to give his marching orders off the rifle squad for poor attendance, but this was not the time and place), the CID lad, and myself. The villain or target had been known to us over a period of eighteen months; he always used a motorcycle during his escapes after a robbery and was known to carry a sawn-off shotgun, which he had fired over the heads of anyone chasing him.

We went to the location and en route called at a fish shop. Bill went into the shop and ordered for himself and the other two. I declined as I had already eaten at home. Bill got into a row with a woman who complained about police doing as they liked. She was referring to our young CID driver who had driven down a one-way street the wrong way and parked outside the shop. I had already spoken to the lad and told him to turn the car around, which he did. I went into the shop and heard Bill still shouting at this lady. He pointed out to her he had been on duty since 8 a.m. and now was on his way to face an armed robber, and the fish and chips may well be his last meal as any one of us could be killed in order to protect people like her. I left the shop fuming. We arrived on site and decided a plan of action.

We were parked up and waiting for the target to arrive. We were having radio problems and changed our position several times. Bill's temper had not eased up, and he and I clashed again. We were equal in rank, so he could not order me about. I told him if he did not ease up on the other two, I would abort the whole job. This quietened him down, and we waited in silence.

The target arrived on plot and parked his motorcycle two cars away from us. He dismounted and took off his black motorcycle jacket and put on another brown jacket. He also carried a plastic bag in his right hand. He left his bike and went to pick up the proceeds of the robberies he had committed earlier. When he was clear, I left our car and disabled his motorbike by removing the plug leads.

To be continued in volume 2.

Lightning Source UK Ltd.
Milton Keynes UK
UKHW010848080320
359884UK00009B/44